the**bush**theatre

CW00358193

# FLIGHT PATH

## by David Watson

**12 September - 6 October**
**Bush Theatre, London**
020 7610 4224   www.bushtheatre.co.uk

**9 – 13 October**
**The REP, Birmingham**
0121 236 4455   www.birmingham-rep.co.uk

**15 & 16 October**
**Trinity Theatre, Tunbridge Wells**
01892 678 678   www.trinitytheatre.net

**18 - 20 October**
**Sherman Theatre, Cardiff**
029 2064 6900   www.shermantheatre.co.uk

**30 & 31 October**
**Wakefield Arts Centre**
01924 211 311   www.theatreroyalwakefield.co.uk

**2 & 3 November**
**Mill Studio, Yvonne Arnaud Theatre, Guildford**
01483 44 00 00   www.yvonne-arnaud.co.uk

**6 – 10 November**
**Traverse Theatre, Edinburgh**
0131 228 1404   www.traverse.co.uk

*Flight Path* was first performed at The Bush Theatre, London, on 12 September 2007, in a co-production between Out of Joint and The Bush Theatre.

## CAST:

| | |
|---|---|
| Sean | **Will Knightley** |
| Jonathan | **Cary Crankson** |
| Daniel | **Scott Swadkins** |
| Joe | **Jason Maza** |
| Lauren | **Ashley Madekwe** |
| Susan | **Mossie Smith** |

| | |
|---|---|
| Director | **Naomi Jones** |
| Designer | **Polly Sullivan** |
| Lighting Designer | **Natasha Chivers** |
| Sound Designer | **Carolyn Downing** |
| Costume Supervisor | **Sydney Florence** |
| Fight Director | **Paul Benzing** |

| | |
|---|---|
| Production Manager | **Gary Beestone** |
| Company Stage Manager | **Richard Llewelyn** |
| Assistant Stage Manager | **Liv Jolliffe** (tour) |
| Production Photographer | **Graham Michael** |
| Carer | **David Moore** |

With grateful thanks to Ruth Piggott at Mind the Gap
theatre company, Spare Tyre theatre company, and Kathy
Davis at Forward 4 Work (Birmingham City Council).

# COMPANY AND CREATIVE TEAM

**NATASHA CHIVERS**
**Lighting Designer**

Recent work includes:
2007 Olivier Award for Best
Lighting Design for *Sunday
In The Park With George*
(Wyndhams Theatre); *Beyond
Belief* (Legs On The Wall at
The Carriageworks, Sydney);
*Ballet for The People* (Royal
Festival Hall/Ballet Boyz); *That
Face* (Jerwood Royal Court
Theatre Upstairs); *Wolves
In The Walls* (Improbable/
National Theatre Scotland);
*Encore* (George Piper Dances
-Sadlers Wells/tour); *Pool (No
Water)* (Frantic Assembly);
*HOME Glasgow* and *Mary
Stuart* (National Theatre
Scotland); *Kindertransport*
(Shared Experience). Other
work includes: *Palace
Dreams* and *Renaissance*
(Greenwich and Docklands
International Festival);
*Dirty Wonderland* (Frantic
Assembly/Brighton Festival);
*Hymns, Peepshow* and *Tiny
Dynamite* (Frantic Assembly,
Lyric Hammersmith,
National/International
tours); *Jerusalem, Playhouse
Creatures* (West Yorkshire
Playhouse); *Mercury Fur*
(with Plymouth Drum), *Small
Things*, and *Pyrenees* (with
The Tron Theatre Glasgow),
*The Straits* (59 East 59, New
York, Hampstead Theatre/
Paines Plough); *The Bomb-
itty of Errors* (West End) and
*A Fine Balance* (Tamasha
-Hampstead Theatre/tour).

**GRAHAM COWLEY**
**Producer**

Out of Joint's Producer since
1998. His long collaboration
with Max Stafford-Clark

began as Joint Stock Theatre
Group's first General Manager
for seven years in the 1970s.
He was General Manager
of the Royal Court for eight
years, and on their behalf
transferred a string of hit
plays to the West End. His
career has spanned the full
range of theatre production,
from small fringe companies
to major West End shows
and large scale commercial
tours. Outside Out of
Joint, he has produced the
notorious *Harry and Me* at
the Warehouse Theatre
and his own translation of
*End of Story* at the Chelsea
Theatre. The fiercely anti-
war *Forgotten Voices from
the Great War* season at
the Pleasance Theatre was
followed by *What the Women
Did* (Southwark Playhouse,
September 2004) and *Red
Night*, by James Lansdale
Hodson (Finborough,
November 2005). *My Real
War 1914-?*, based on the
letters of a young WW1
soldier, enjoyed a successful
tour in Spring 2007 and tours
again from October 2007.

**CARY CRANKSON**
**Jonathan**

Cary trained at RADA. His
**theatre** includes *Silverland*

(Lacuna Theatre.Co/New
York); *Coriolanus* (Brockley
Jack Theatre); *Medea*
(Bridewell Theatre); *Othello*
(Love & Madness); Romeo
in *Romeo & Juliet* (Lost
Theatre); *The Fall* (Young Vic).
**Television** includes *Doctors*.
**Films** include *Underneath*
and *You're Gonna Wake Up
One Morning* (Empire Film
Award for Best Short Film).

**CAROLYN DOWNING**
**Sound Designer**

Carolyn's designs include
*Absurdia* (Donmar
Warehouse); *Alaska* (Royal
Court); *Topdog Underdog*
(Sheffield Crucible Studio);
the recent revival of *Angels
in America* (Headlong, Lyric
Hammersmith, Citizens
Glasgow); *The Winter's Tale,
Pericles, Days of Significance*
(Royal Shakespeare
Company); *A Whistle in
the Dark, Moonshed* (Royal
Exchange, Manchester);
*Hysteria* (Inspector Sands/
Stamping Ground Theatre);
*Project D: I'm Mediocre* (The
Work Theatre Collective);
*Arsenic and Old Lace* (Derby
Playhouse); *The Water Engine*
(Theatre 503/Young Vic);
*Blood Wedding* (Almeida);
*Gone to Earth* (Shared
Experience); *Waiting for
the Parade* (Mountview
Academy of Theatre Arts);
*Habitats, Under the Curse*
(Gate Theatre); *Stallerhof, A
Doll's House, The Double Bass,
The Provoked Wife, Mongoose*
(Southwark Playhouse); *The
Watery Part of the World*
(Sound & Fury). Carolyn was
associate sound designer
on *The Overwhelming* (in

association with Out of Joint) and *Fix Up* (both National Theatre); *O go my Man* (Out of Joint/Royal Court); *Macbeth* (Out of Joint, UK & International Tour); *Forty Winks* (Royal Court) and *By the Bog of Cats* (Wyndham's Theatre). She was Assistant to the Sound Designer on *Billy Elliot: the Musical* and number one sound operator on *Blood Brothers* (Phoenix Theatre).

**NAOMI JONES**
**Director**

Naomi recently directed *Machinal* (Oxford School of Drama at BAC); *One Million Tiny Plays About London* (Clerkenwell Theatre); and *After Miss Julie* (GEST, Sweden); as well as the revival of Russell Barr's hit *Sisters, Such Devoted Sisters* (Drill Hall). As Assistant Director at Out of Joint Naomi has worked on *Duck, The Permanent Way, Macbeth, Talking to Terrorists, O go my Man* and *King of Hearts*.

**WILL KNIGHTLEY**
**Sean**

Will appeared in *The Permanent Way* for Out of Joint (Sydney & UK tour, a co-production with the National

Theatre) and was previously at The Bush in *Crimes of the Heart*. Other **theatre** includes *Cinderella* (Oxford Playhouse); *Lone Star Mark 3, Sleuth, The Tempest* (Salisbury Playhouse); *Our Country's Good, Cyrano De Bergerac* (Nuffield, Southampton); *The Crucible* (Centreline/tour); *School for Scandal* (English Touring Theatre); *Dracula* (Cheltenham Everyman); *Woman in Mind* (Palace Watford & USA); *Death and the Maiden* (Library, Manchester); *Hush* (Royal Court); *Oedipus Tyrannos* (Contact, Manchester); *Romeo and Juliet* (Lyceum, Edinburgh); *The Triumph of Love, Summerfolk* (Minerva, Chichester); *Diplomatic Wives* (Palace, Watford); *The Three Musketeers* (New Vic Company Tour); *Macbeth* (Bristol Old Vic); *Wild Honey* (National Theatre); *Lazy Days* (Theatre Royal, Stratford East); *Sus* (Soho Poly); *Brothers Karamazov* (Fortune); *Hamlet* (Royal Court); *Fanshen, Light Shining in Buckinghamshire, Yesterday's News, A Mad World My Masters, Epsom Downs* (Joint Stock). **Television** includes *City of Vice; Charles I & the Regicides; Rosemary & Thyme; The Brief; Heartbeat; Foyle's War; Midsomer Murders; The Project; Inspector Linley Mysteries; Without Motive II; Meat Extract; Kavanagh QC; The Bill; Peak Practice; The Bill; No Bananas; Cracker; A Touch of Frost; Casualty; Harry; Goodbye Cruel World; Close Relations; Oscar Wilde; The Hound of the Baskervilles; Electric in the City.* **Films** include *The Mill on the Floss; Dinosaur* and *Skinflicker.*

**ASHLEY MADEKWE**
**Lauren**

**THEATRE**
Ashley graduated from RADA in 2005. Her **theatre** includes *The Indian Boy* (Royal Shakespeare Company); *93.2FM* (Royal Court); *The Prayer Room* (Edinburgh Lyceum/Birmingham Rep); *Little Sweet Thing* (Hampstead Theatre/Tour). **Television** includes *Drop Dead Gorgeous II; Prime Suspect; Vital Signs; Teachers; Hope and Glory.* **Films** include *How To Lose Friends and Alienate People; Cassandra's Dream; Venus* and *Storm Damage.*

**JASON MAZA**
**Joe**

Jason's **theatre** includes *The Cage* (Nuffield Theatre) and

Gutted and Taken In (Tristan Bates Theatre). **Television** appearances include My Boy Jack, The Bill, The Lawrences, Holby City, Casualty, Life Begins and Eastenders. **Films** include Rise of the Foot Soldier, Special People, Dolphins, Outlaw, Brick It, Life n Lyrics, Hush Your Mouth and Pit.

**MOSSIE SMITH**
**Susan**

Mossie previously appeared with Out of Joint in O go my Man (co-produced with the Royal Court). Other theatre includes Longitude (Greenwich theatre); Getting to the Foot of the Mountain (Birmingham Rep); Howard Katz, Wild Oats (National Theatre); Road, Shirley, The Recruiting Officer, Our Country's Good, Three Birds Alighting on a Field (Royal Court); Sex Please, We're Italian, The Crucible (Young Vic); Blithe Spirit (Bromley); Babes in the Wood (Salisbury Playhouse); See How They Run (Canterbury); and Oh Dear Purcell! (Stationers Hall). **Television** includes regular appearances as Aunt Megan in Hearts of Gold and Petula Belcher in The Riff-Raff Element. Other

appearances include 2000 Streets Under the Sky, In Deep, The Bill, Midsomer Murders, Undercover Heart, Goodnight Mr. Tom, Tom Jones, Rough Justice, French and Saunders, Harry Enfield and Chums, The Widowing of Mrs. Holroyd, Absolutely Fabulous, Casualty, Prime Suspect I and IV, Heroes and Villains, Mr Wakefield's Crusade, Queen of the East, Come Home Charlie and Face Them, A Very Peculiar Practice, Road, Putting on the Ritz, Rat in the Skull, South of the Border, Wuffer, Reith, Give us a Break, Number 10, I'm a Stranger Here Myself, Woman in White and Tiny Revolutions. **Films** include Flick, House, Breathtaking, Janice Beard 45 wpm, The Girl with Brains in her Feet, Up the Valley, Second Best and Memoirs of a Survivor. **Radio:** Desmond Oliver Dingle's Complete Life and Works of William Shakespeare.

**POLLY SULLIVAN**
**Designer**

Polly recently designed Naomi Jones' production of Machinal (BAC/Oxford School of Drama). Other theatre designs include Called to Account and How Long Is Never? Darfur - A Response (Tricycle); The Atheist (Theatre 503); You Might As Well Live (New End Theatre); Free The Lady – Aung San Suu Kyi and The 24 Hour plays (The Old Vic); Seduced (Finborough Theatre); and The Snow Dragon (US tour, UK tour, Soho Theatre).

**SCOTT SWADKINS**
**Daniel**

Flight Path is Scott's first theatre role. Most recently he appeared in the film Special People (also with Jason Maza) which premiered at the 2007 Edinburgh International Film Festival. In 2001, Scott joined Forward 4 Work, a key part of Disability Employment Services within Birmingham City Council. He gained a number of qualifications with work placements at a book shop at The Custard Factory in Birmingham and the city's Nature Centre. Scott began acting in King Fu, made by 104 Films as part of their series DisLife made by people with disabilities. The following year he played the lead in their film The Dance Off. Scott is very excited at taking this opportunity to become a professional actor.

**DAVID WATSON**
**Writer**

David Watson's first play, Just A Bloke, was staged as part of the Royal Court's Young Writers Festival when he was just 17. He is a graduate of Birmingham Repertory Theatre's Transmissions scheme for young writers.

out of joint

**"You expect something special from the touring company Out of Joint"**
The Times

Out of Joint is a national and international touring theatre company dedicated to the development and production of new writing. Under the direction of Max Stafford-Clark the company has premiered plays from leading writers including David Hare, Caryl Churchill, Alistair Beaton, Sebastian Barry and Timberlake Wertenbaker, as well as introducing first-time writers such as Simon Bennett, Stella Feehily and Mark Ravenhill.

**"Max Stafford-Clark's excellent Out of Joint company"**
The Independent

Touring all over the UK, Out of Joint frequently performs at and co-produces with key venues such as the Royal Court and the National Theatre. The company has performed in six continents – most recently a world tour of its award-winning, Africa-inspired *Macbeth*. Back home, Out of Joint also pursues an extensive education programme.

**"Out of Joint is out of this world"**
Boston Globe

PRODUCTIONS TO DATE
2007 *King of Hearts* 2006 *The Overwhelming* (NT in association with OjO); *O go my Man* by Stella Feehily 2005 *Talking to Terrorists* by Robin Soans 2004 *Macbeth* by William Shakespeare; *Sisters, Such Devoted Sisters* by Russell Barr 2003 *The Permanent Way* by David Hare; *Duck* by Stella Feehily 2002 *A Laughing Matter* by April De Angelis & *She Stoops to Conquer* by Oliver Goldsmith; *Hinterland* by Sebastian Barry 2001 *Sliding with Suzanne* by Judy Upton; *Feelgood* by Alistair Beaton 2000 *Rita, Sue and Bob Too* by Andrea Dunbar & *A State Affair* by Robin Soans 1999 *Some Explicit Polaroids* by Mark Ravenhill; *Drummers* by Simon Bennett 1998 *Our Country's Good* by Timberlake Wertenbaker; *Our Lady of Sligo* by Sebastian Barry 1997 *Blue Heart* by Caryl Churchill; *The Positive Hour* by April De Angelis 1996 *Shopping and Fucking* by Mark Ravenhill 1995 *The Steward of Christendom* by Sebastian Barry; *Three Sisters* by Anton Chekhov & *The Break of Day* by Timberlake Wertenbaker 1994 *The Man of Mode* by George Etherege & *The Libertine* by Stephen Jeffreys; *The Queen and I* by Sue Townsend & *Road* by Jim Cartwright

Photos by John Haynes: *O go my Man*; *The Queen and I*; *Shopping & Fucking*

## THE COMPANY

| | |
|---|---|
| Director | **Max Stafford-Clark** |
| Producer | **Graham Cowley** |
| Marketing Manager | **Jon Bradfield** |
| Administrator and Education Manager | **Rebecca Pilbeam** |
| Assistant Director & PA to Artistic Director | **Naomi Jones** |
| Literary Manager | **Alex Roberts** |
| Finance Officer | **Sandra Palumbo** |

## Board of Directors

Kate Ashfield, Linda Bassett, John Blackmore (Chair), Elyse Dodgson, Sonia Friedman, Stephen Jeffreys, Paul Jesson, Danny Sapani, Karl Sydow

## OjO education work

Out of Joint offers a diverse programme of workshops and discussions for groups coming to see our performances. For full details of our education programme, resource packs or Our Country's Good workshops, contact Rebecca at Out of Joint.

## Out of Joint

| | |
|---|---|
| Post: | 7 Thane Works, Thane Villas, London N7 7NU |
| Tel: | 020 7609 0207 |
| Fax: | 020 7609 0203 |
| Email: | ojo@outofjoint.co.uk |
| Website: | www.outofjoint.co.uk |

**Out of Joint is grateful to the following for their support over the years:**
Arts Council England, The Foundation for Sport and the Arts, The Baring Foundation, The Paul Hamlyn Foundation, The Olivier Foundation, The Peggy Ramsay Foundation, The John S Cohen Foundation, The David Cohen Charitable Trust, The National Lottery through the Arts Council of England, The Prudential Awards, Stephen Evans, Karl Sydow, Harold Stokes and Friends of Theatre, John Lewis Partnership, Royal Victoria Hall Foundation. Out of Joint is a registered charity 1033059

## KEEP IN TOUCH

For information on our shows, tour details and offers, get in touch (contact details above) letting us know whether you'd like to receive information by post or email.

## BOOKSHOP

Scripts like this one are available for many of our previous shows at exclusive discounted prices from our online shop www.outofjoint.co.uk

# thebushtheatre

*"One of the most experienced prospectors of raw talent in Europe"*
The Independent

The Bush Theatre is one of the most celebrated new writing theatres in the world. We have an international reputation for discovering, nurturing and producing the best new theatre writers from the widest range of backgrounds, and for presenting their work to the highest possible standards. We look for exciting new voices that tell contemporary stories with wit, style and passion and we champion work that is both provocative and entertaining.

With around 40,000 people enjoying our productions each year, The Bush has produced hundreds of ground-breaking premieres since its inception 35 years ago. The theatre produces up to eight productions of new plays a year, many of them Bush commissions, and hosts guest productions by leading companies and artists from all over the world.

*"When it comes to plays that capture the detail of ordinary lives and the still, sad and often wonderfully comic music of humanity, The Bush is in a class of its own"* Daily Telegraph

The Bush is widely acclaimed as the seedbed for the best new playwrights, many of whom have gone on to become established names in the entertainment industry, including Steve Thompson, Jack Thorne, Amelia Bullmore, Dennis Kelly, Chloë Moss, David Eldridge, Stephen Poliakoff, Snoo Wilson, Terry Johnson, Kevin Elyot, Doug Lucie, Dusty Hughes, Sharman Macdonald, Billy Roche, Catherine Johnson, Philip Ridley, Richard Cameron, Jonathan Harvey, Conor McPherson, Joe Penhall, Helen Blakeman, Mark O'Rowe and Charlotte Jones.

The Bush Theatre provides a free script reading service, receiving over 1000 scripts through the post every year, and reading them all. This is one small part of a comprehensive **Writers' Development Programme**, which includes workshops, one-to-one dramaturgy, rehearsed readings, research bursaries, masterclasses, residencies and commissions. We have also launched a pilot scheme for an ambitious new education, training and professional development programme, **bushfutures**, providing opportunities for different sectors of the community and professionals to access the expertise of Bush writers, directors, designers, technicians and actors, and to play an active role in influencing the future development of the theatre and its programme.

The Bush Theatre is extremely proud of its reputation for artistic excellence, its friendly atmosphere, and its undisputed role as a major force in shaping the future of British theatre.

**www.bushtheatre.co.uk**

supported by
**h&f**
hammersmith & fulham

ARTS COUNCIL ENGLAND

**Be There at the Beginning**
Join as a patron member and you will be closely involved in discovering the most important and exciting playwrights of the future. Patron membership levels start at only £100. For an information pack please call 020 7602 3703 or visit www.bushtheatre.co.uk

## The Bush Theatre
Shepherds Bush Green
London W12 8QD

Box Office: 020 7610 4224
www.bushtheatre.co.uk

# THE YATTY'S WHERE IT'S ATTY

- some vocabulary

| | |
|---|---|
| shanks | makeshift knife |
| muggy | dull, daft, crap |
| mug someone off | take the piss out of |
| yat | female, a girl/woman |
| buzzin | really happy/stoned/high |
| reach | to be bothered |
| mish | abv: mission, something difficult |
| touch | stroke of luck |
| neekos | from neek - cross btw nerd and geek |
| what's poppin | what's up? |
| lick-shot | good piece of music |
| boy off | to be rude to or ignore or to walk away from someone |
| batty hole | arse hole |
| floss it out | show something off / act flamboyantly |
| ute ("yoot") | youth |
| blood-clart | blood clot |
| on the ones | alone, to be on one's own |
| waste | useless, waste of space |

- for an extensive look at slang, visit **www.urbandictionary.com**

# David Watson
## Flight Path
### *and*
## Undercarriage

**ff**

*faber and faber*

First published in 2007
by Faber and Faber Limited
3 Queen Square, London WCIN 3AU

Typeset by Country Setting, Kingsdown, Kent CT14 8ES
Printed in the UK by CPI Bookmarque, Croydon, CR0 4TD

A CIP record for this book
is available from the British Library

ISBN 978-0-571-23918-4

2 4 6 8 10 9 7 5 3 1

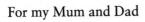
For my Mum and Dad

# Contents

# FLIGHT PATH

# Acknowledgements

Many thanks to Ramin Gray, Simon Stephens,
Mel Kenyon, Carl Miller, Suzanne Gorman, Naomi Jones
and all at Out of Joint, Josie Rourke and all at the Bush,
for their help and encouragement in the writing of this play.
Also to Noel Greig, Ben Payne, Caroline Jester and
all at Birmingham Rep, and to all the staff at the
Royal Court Young Writers' Programme.

# Characters

**Jonathan**
eighteen

**Daniel**
twenty-five, his brother,
who has Down's syndrome

**Sean**
their father, fifties

**Susan**
their mother, fifties

**Joe**
eighteen

**Lauren**
seventeen

The play takes place in London,
between January and December 2007.

The characters are all Londoners, although Sean
is Scottish and speaks with a soft Scots accent.

The dialogue is written as it should be spoken,
so punctuation often appears in, odd places.

A / stroke in the dialogue indicates the point
where the next speaker interrupts and overlaps
with the first, or where the next stage direction occurs.

*This text went to press before the end of rehearsals,
so may differ slightly from the play as performed.*

## ONE

*January.*
   *Sean's new office, in a university building. It's a bit of a tip, with boxes all over the place.*
   *Sean is pacing, on the phone.*

**Sean** (*phone*) *Back to the Future.* /

   *Knocks on the door.*

(*Phone. Opening door.*) Yeah *Back to the F–* , *Back to –* John!

**Jonathan** (*entering*) How you / doing.

**Sean** (*phone*) With the car there and everything there's a, a thesis in it trust me – I won't be a minute /

**Jonathan** Yeah /

**Sean** (*phone, laughs*) Yeah, yeah, well you . . . well you do that Well look I have to go. I do. OK but I'll, what's your . . . yeah. Well I'll see you next week then. OK. Thanks Rachel bye-bye now. (*Hangs up*) That was incredibly rude / of me I was I should've . . . well I shouldn't have really have . . .

**Jonathan** No no it was I was, I'm only . . . It's . . . Who was it?

**Sean** Er that was a . . . student Well anyway, John!

   *Beat.*

– athan. (*Beat.*) How are you Happy New / Year

**Jonathan** Happy New Year /

**Sean**  How are you What's happening What's the crack? Geezer?

*Beat.*

**Jonathan**  I don't know Dad what is the crack?

**Sean**  Are you well?

**Jonathan**  (*nodding*) I'm . . . cold.

**Sean**  You've got a cold?

**Jonathan**  No I am, cold /

**Sean**  You are cold well I was gonna say I've got a . . . er but never mind you got my text?

**Jonathan**  Yeah I got that / yeah

**Sean**  Oh you did get that /

**Jonathan**  Yeah I got that yeah I /

**Sean**  Right yeah I was worrying er . . . Well anyway as you see I'm . . .

*He indicates the office around him.*

**Jonathan**  Er, Yes it's a bit . . . messy

**Sean**  Messy is not the fucking word I wanted to get a . . . y'know one a' those . . .

*He mimes a baggage-trolley type thing.*

**Jonathan**  One a' those . . . ?

**Sean**  But no it's . . . boxes it's . . . all the way it's /

**Jonathan**  Yeah yeah.

**Sean**  (*distracted*) And this particular box . . . er Sit down.

**Jonathan**  (*indicating door*) Oh no I'm /

12

**Sean** (*moving a box*) Should probably belong . . . (*Exits, off.*) Would you like a drink?

**Jonathan** Er . . .

**Sean** (*re-entering*) I should tell you the culinary . . . facilities are rather /

**Jonathan** Yeah I only really come in to er . . . . (*Beat.*) So the champagne's on . . . ice, then or what, is it.

   *Beat.*

**Sean** Er, Well /

**Jonathan** Professor. (*Beat.*) Do I call you Professor now.

   *Beat.*

**Sean** Well you can . . . (*call me anything you want*).

   *Beat. Sean indicates a window.*

Er, East. (*Beat.*) Canary Wharf The rolling . . . Essex, flatlands. (*Other window.*) West. The city, the money.

   *Jonathan half-laughs.*

'S my . . . office, penthouse.

**Jonathan** Is it.

**Sean** It is. Er, A south . . . facing would've been . . .

**Jonathan** Yeah.

**Sean** . . . er but life, as they say, is compromise.

**Jonathan** Sure is.

   *Pause. Sean opens his mouth to speak, but Jonathan cuts in.*

**Jonathan** So Danny's coming back then. (*Beat.*) Monday . . . Tuesday week.

*Pause.*

**Sean**  Yes. (*Beat.*) Yes. Now, er . . . Sit down.

*Beat. Jonathan starts to sit down.*

Er Because I have been meaning to . . . How's . . . tricks how's . . . school?

**Jonathan**  Sixth Form / College

**Sean**  College, College.

*Beat.*

**Jonathan**  (*nods*) College is . . . it's OK.

**Sean**  A-ha?

*Beat.*

**Jonathan**  Yeah I swear it's getting more . . .

**Sean**  You're working hard?

**Jonathan**  I'm . . .

**Sean**  Ha?

**Jonathan**  No I am, I am. (*Beat.*) I am.

**Sean**  And your friends are working hard?

*Jonathan half-laughs, shrugs.*

They're playing hard are you playing hard?

**Jonathan**  (*half-laughs*) Boy.

**Sean**  There's er . . . Listen to this There's two types of student, right There's the one . . . who'll turn up at your door, after the seminar y'know there's a knock at the er . . . at the door 'I really enjoyed the seminar Professor would you read over me essay notes for me,' 'Oh yeah yeah,' and the *other* . . . who . . . who comes . . . what is it he comes . . . There's two types of student there's the one who . . . who er . . .

*He's forgotten. Beat. Jonathan starts to laugh, quietly.*

Er . . . well bollocks anyway there's two . . . (*Laughing.*) there's two types of er . . . of student . . .

**Jonathan** (*still laughing*) Danny . . .

**Sean** And and they're both . . .

**Jonathan** Danny had a knife. (*Beat.*) Put in his face. (*Beat.*) By a . . . y'know by some spastic. (*Beat.*) Up there.

*Beat. The phone rings. Sean quickly picks it up and slams it down again. Beat. He half-laughs. Jonathan stares at him. Pause.*

**Sean** Is . . . does your mum . . .

*Beat.*

**Jonathan** I'd better / go

**Sean** Y'know this hasn't been . . . the easiest of . . . for me either, y'know? (*Beat.*) But I'm, I'm . . .

*Beat.*

**Jonathan** I should gotta . . . make a / move

**Sean** Oh now come on now gimme / a

**Jonathan** No I'm, I'm /

**Sean** The kettle's boiled it's green tea I've got some green tea. Keep out the cold.

*Beat.*

**Jonathan** I /

**Sean** Have a f– . . . drink with your dad.

*Pause.*

**Jonathan** Well if it's . . . green tea then . . .

**Sean** That's the stuff.

*Sean exits. Jonathan starts hurriedly going through his dad's wallet.*

(*Off.*) That's the stuff I was worried . . . actually that you wouldn't get through the front door /

**Jonathan** Oh yeah?

**Sean** (*off*) Strictly it's it's . . . it's Christmas around here y'see, still, er . . .

*Jonathan has found a photo of someone. He quickly stuffs it in his pocket as Sean re-enters.*

Here we are. Er now that's . . . hot /

*Jonathan takes a big gulp anyway and stares at Sean, half-smiling. Beat. Sean clears his throat.*

How's . . . the Airport?

**Jonathan** Yep, still standing.

**Sean** And Joe. Joe? Joe.

**Jonathan** Yeah he's . . . still standing too.

*Beat.*

**Sean** And the work's . . . interesting?

**Jonathan** Not really no It's boring, it's very boring.

*Beat. Sean laughs.*

**Sean** Is it not quite a long way to go? Er, for a job that is so . . . (*Beat.*) Well anyway it's . . . January . . . now, you must have your . . . predicted . . .

**Jonathan** Three As one B.

**Sean** Three As one . . . Oh well that's, that's . . . what's . . . the B for?

**Jonathan** Economics.

**Sean** OK. (*Beat.*) OK. Well that's . . . (*Raises his cup to him, drinks. Beat.*) You can make it four As.

**Jonathan** Most people only do three. (*Beat.*) Y'know they do three. (*Beat.*) A levels.

*Beat.*

**Sean** Well why d'you think that is? (*Beat.*) Ha?

*Pause.*

**Jonathan** Four As.

**Sean** (*touching cups*) Four As you can do it.

**Jonathan** Yep.

**Sean** You can do it If a job's worth doing. (*Beat.*) Y'know?

*Jonathan nods, obligingly. Beat.*

Er . . .

**Jonathan** (*indicating picture*) St Ives.

*Beat.*

**Sean** Yes. I f– . . . Of course you remember /

**Jonathan** Yeah I do remember / yeah

**Sean** Summer 19 . . . 98 would you believe and Danny on the . . . surfboard and your mother . . .

**Jonathan** Yeah /

**Sean** on the Pinot Grigiot most of the time if I recall It was, It was . . .

**Jonathan** Yeah it was . . . good, then.

*Pause.*

**Sean** Er, So now you know . . . (*Indicates the office around him.*) Er, will you come . . . will I see you around . . . more often?

*Pause.*

**Jonathan** Well will we see you. Around. More often.
(*Beat.*) Because Danny's . . . coming back and I'm . . .

*Pause.*

**Sean** Er, Well, I mean, It's . . . (*Half-laughs.*) Everyone's . . .
got . . . I'm . . . trying to . . . Of course I . . .

*Pause.*

**Jonathan** Gotta make a move.

**Sean** You've /

**Jonathan** I've gotta go college

**Sean** Oh well there's no rest for the . . . for the wicked /

**Jonathan** Well there's no rest for the . . . people who got
college anyway /

**Sean** Right yeah . . . Oh before you go!

*Searches for something.*

I've got a . . . something for you . . . err . . . Ha!

*Hands him a flyer. Beat.*

**Jonathan** Oh.

*Sean half-laughs.*

The book launch.

**Sean** *The.* (*Beat.*) Book launch. (*Beat.*) It's . . . St John
Street it's round the corner it's down the road. (*Beat.*) So
you must . . .

**Jonathan** Yeah I'll . . . sounds . . .

**Sean** You'll pencil it in.

**Jonathan** I'll do that.

*Beat. Sean awkwardly embraces Jonathan. Beat.*

**Sean** You'll take care.

**Jonathan** (*half-laughs*) Yeah.

*Beat.*

**Sean** (*indicating door*) I'll . . .

**Jonathan** No I'm . . .

**Sean** It's /

**Jonathan** No you don't have to You don't have to You
don't have to. (*Beat.*) I'll . . .

*Beat.*

**Sean** / Yeah.

**Jonathan** Yeah

*Blackout. In the blackout, Jonathan tears up the flyer
and discards it. Meanwhile, Daniel enters, and starts
carefully doing his hair, as if in front of a mirror.*


TWO

*February.*
    *Jonathan's living room. Morning.*
    *Jonathan is just closing the door behind him. He
carries a sports bag, out of which protrudes a fluorescent
jacket.*
    *He turns the light on, and jumps as he sees Daniel.*

**Jonathan** Jesus f– Christ /

**Daniel** (*laughing*) What's, What's the matter with you?

**Jonathan** What you doing standing in the dark?

**Daniel** I wanted, I wanted to scare you.

**Jonathan** Oh well you f– . . . You did that What you do–
You're not suppos– You're supposed to be at the doctor's.

**Daniel** What?

**Jonathan** Why aren't you at the d– . . . Oh J– Why aren't
you at the doctor's?

**Daniel** Well, Mum said . . .

*Beat.*

**Jonathan** What?

*Beat.*

**Daniel** That she couldn't actually take me today any
more.

*Jonathan picks up the phone.*

Because, Because something came up at work.

*Jonathan stares at him.*

What?

*Beat. Jonathan sighs.*

**Jonathan** Well you're here now The boy's back in town.

**Daniel** Shut up.

**Jonathan** Quarter to eight You gave me a shock.

**Daniel** I know I did. You silly bitch.

**Jonathan** Come again?

**Daniel** (*laughing*) You heard.

*Beat.*

**Jonathan** I missed you Danny.

**Daniel** Did you really?

*Beat.*

**Jonathan** Course I did Put it there.

**Daniel** Yeah I miss, I missed, I missed you too

**Jonathan** Yeah put it there like.

*Daniel starts to shake Jonathan's hand, but Jonathan corrects him.*

No no it's . . . Like that like. Like the Somali boys do it. You can be a Somali boy.

**Daniel** Cool.

**Jonathan** No it's not that . . . cool but anyway you're back around You're back in the endz bruv.

**Daniel** (*laughing*) Stop it.

**Jonathan** Yeah you got back last night?

**Daniel** Yeah ten, Ten forty-two, at London Euston.

**Jonathan** Oh wow Did you come back on the tube then?

**Daniel** Me – Me and Mum did yeah.

**Jonathan** Or did you get the bus?

**Daniel** Me – Me and Mum did yeah.

*Beat.*

**Jonathan** What you got the tube or the bus?

*Beat.*

**Daniel** I can hardly remember.

*Jonathan smiles.*

**Jonathan** Course not.

**Daniel** I'm ac– I'm actually really really glad that I'm here. And not there.

*Beat.*

**Jonathan** Did you manage to make . . . any more . . . friends?

**Daniel** Not really no. (*Beat.*) I mean . . . I mean some . . . I mean some of them were alright but . . . most of them were just . . . bitches and fuckers.

**Jonathan** Right.

*Beat. Daniel smiles.*

**Daniel** I actually swear quite a lot don't I?

**Jonathan** (*smiles*) You do a bit you cunt yeah.

**Daniel** Well I've actually learnt something else new as well.

**Jonathan** Oh yeah what's . . .

*Daniel straightens his back, then proudly gobs on the floor.*

What d'you do that for?

**Daniel** (*laughing*) What!

**Jonathan** (*moving to clear it up*) That's disgusting.

**Daniel** (*smiling*) No it's not. You're disgusting. Dog. You're a dog aren't you?

**Jonathan** No I'm not.

**Daniel** (*laughing*) Yes you are.

*Jonathan kneels on the floor to wipe the spit.*

**Jonathan** Listen now that you're back here . . .

*Daniel laughs, reaching down and resting his hand on his brother's head.*

What you doing?

**Daniel** (*laughs*) Nothing.

**Jonathan** (*rising to his feet*) What are you doing?

**Daniel** Nothing.

**Jonathan** Come on.

*Jonathan starts brushing Daniel's hand away, but each time he does so Daniel puts his other hand up on his face, laughing.*

No come on come on. Stop it.

*Daniel laughs more.*

Stop it.

*Jonathan punches Daniel in the face. Daniel clutches his nose. Beat.*

Look what you . . .

*Jonathan exits. Beat. He re-enters with a damp tissue.*

Here. (*Brushing his hand away.*) Move, here.

*Pause.*

**Daniel** Thanks. (*Beat.*) I'm sorry about that.

**Jonathan** No I'm sorry.

**Daniel** No I'm sorry.

**Jonathan** (*aggressive*) No I'm sorry.

*Jonathan stops himself. Pause.*

**Daniel** The only thing . . . that I actually liked . . . about . . . about Ravenscroft . . . was the gardening.

*Beat.*

**Jonathan** Oh well that's . . . Well sorry about that 'cos we haven't got a . . .

**Daniel** Because I helped to plant . . . a rose. And a heather. And a rhod– and a rhododendron.

**Jonathan** That's . . . very nice . . . Daniel let's . . .

**Daniel** Mum said that we should go and see a film.

*Beat.*

**Jonathan** What?

**Daniel** (*producing a note*) And then we should go to Londis to get something for lunch, and then we should go and take me to the doctor's.

*Beat.*

**Jonathan** It's eight o'clock in the morning.

**Daniel** Oh. Well what, Well what are we gonna do?

**Jonathan** What are *we* gonna do? (*Beat. He half-laughs.*) Danny I'm . . . I'm up all night at work, now I've gotta go to sleep, then I've gotta go to college.

*Beat.*

Y'know I've, I'm . . . You know Dad's gone.

**Daniel** Yeah Mum told me that. (*Beat.*) If I could see . . . If I could see, where Dad was now . . . (*Beat.*) I'd probably punch him. (*Beat.*) And probably kill him. (*Beat.*) Because of what he did to me. And what he did to Mum. And what he did to us.

**Jonathan** What did he do to us?

**Daniel** He raped us.

*Jonathan laughs.*

What?

**Jonathan** Don't . . . say words where you dunno what they mean like /

24

**Daniel** Well it feels like it.

*Jonathan laughs.*

I mean it was his . . . I mean it was his idea for me to go to Ravenscroft. (*Beat.*) And look how the way . . . and look how the way that ended up. (*Beat.*) I mean I'm twenty-four, years of age.

**Jonathan** I know you are.

**Daniel** You're eighteen.

**Jonathan** I know.

**Daniel** I, am, actually, a . . . adult. (*Beat.*) I just . . . I just wanna make my own decisions. (*Beat.*) That's all.

*Pause. Jonathan sighs.*

**Jonathan** Well come on let's . . .

**Daniel** I actually drew a heart. Because, because it's nearly Valentine's Day.

*Beat.*

**Jonathan** That's . . . very good Danny well done.

**Daniel** You can have it.

**Jonathan** I don't . . . Thanks, Thank you.

*Beat.*

**Daniel** I've never had, a hug from you.

*Pause.*

**Jonathan** Let's go out.

*Blackout. In the blackout, a plane passes low overhead.*

# THREE

*March.*

    *A children's playground in the shadow of Heathrow Airport. Dark – very early morning.*

    *Jonathan and Joe. Both have their phones clamped to their ears, but neither are talking on them.*

**Joe** Matthew *Dick?* /

**Jonathan** That's what it says on the notice / board All I . . . seen it on the notice board

**Joe** Everyone's taking the piss out a' me – Answer your phone you dozy cow /

**Jonathan** I can't find this voicemail My brother gives me five / voicemails

**Joe** Matthew Dick Well no wonder he's a dick-splurt He gives *me* the formal warning /

**Jonathan** It's because you were blocking the dollies /

**Joe** Blocking the d– (*Re-dialling.*) I'm gonna kill someone – Blocking the dollies?

**Jonathan** You park the thing up by the loading bay / the dolly cars can't get through.

**Joe** Oh for fu– (*Phone.*) Hello? It's . . . Hello? (*To Jonathan.*) She's gone it's gone.

**Jonathan** Who's gone.

**Joe** What's she trying it for Who gives a shit about the dollies?

**Jonathan** Matthew Dick does /

**Joe** Well Matthew Dick can take his dick and go and play with it Oh here we fucking go (*Phone.*) Yeah about time n' all I been missed calling about a year.

**Jonathan** (*found his voicemail*) Oh here it is like This is /

**Joe** (*phone*) What? What I ca– There's suttin wrong with your phone. (*Switches off.*)

**Jonathan** Five voicemails in the middle a' the night every night

**Joe** Well it's . . . more than I get out a' that little yat I swear down

**Jonathan** Yeah well.

**Joe** Yeah well what If I got a voicemail from her I'd be buzzin like I'd probably knock one out on the fucking strength of it.

**Jonathan** He's twenty-four years old

**Joe** Who is?

**Jonathan** I mean f– . . . 'Selfishness,' she says my mum says But when's the last time / she

**Joe** Formal warning f– What am I *do*ing here like /

**Jonathan** He's my bro– I know he's my brother I mean I had . . . noticed /

**Joe** Like Am I a prick or am I a prick like I spend seven hours chucking suitcases about on planes /

*Jonathan groans.*

I've had endless fucking dr– I ain't even told you 'bout the Milton thing.

**Jonathan** What Milton thing /

**Joe** Oh f– Get on this like I see Danny Milton's brother the other day he's gone 'Look, I know you're sniffin about for suttin, cash-in-hand fucking what-not So what about eight weeks in some brickies yard,' right his uncle's fucking brickies / yard

**Jonathan** Bricki– What d'you – Why d'you wanna . . . piss about /

**Joe** Well we ain't all doing A levels are / we

**Jonathan** Oh don't f– . . . start

**Joe** So I've gone, 'Yeah right Sweet as' I'm all lined up I got me National Insurance on the table, when that arsehole-fucking-prick from Social Services rings up She's gone 'Erm, erm, erm, no, no that's a no-go,' 'cos you can't go fucking doing that 'cos that'll . . . break the . . .

**Jonathan** Conditions of / the Asbo

**Joe** Conditions – It'll break the conditions a' the Asbo

**Jonathan** Well there you go /

**Joe** I mean fuck's sake like Wh– I f– I really fucking need this don't I /

**Jonathan** No you don't /

**Joe** I mean What like You think I'm gonna come . . . all the way out here for the rest a' my / life

**Jonathan** I . . . like it out here y'know I'm . . .

**Joe** Oh shut up You know what You . . . can tell yourself what you want I am telling you now, that I ain't coming back here

**Jonathan** Oh yeah where else you gonna go?

**Joe** How come you didn't come on holiday with us?

*Beat.*

**Jonathan** I'm at college.

**Joe** Take a day off Take a week off Why don't you ever do suttin . . . *good* like. Get a laugh. Draw some yat.

**Jonathan** The yatty's where it's atty /

**Joe** That's what I'm talking about /

**Jonathan** I got . . . A levels, to do I got . . . my brother . . .

**Joe** Swear down y'know I'm thinking some mad thoughts y'know John boy /

**Jonathan** Oh yeah?

**Joe** Progressive like What you doing Sunday?

**Jonathan** Why?

*Pause.*

**Joe** I think it's about time we got on the property ladder like y'understand? /

**Jonathan** (*shaking his head*) Aaaaah /

**Joe** What? What?

**Jonathan** I don't wanna talk about / this

**Joe** 'Aaaah. I don't wanna talk ab–' What's the matter with you like How you living? /

**Jonathan** I'm living alright /

**Joe** No you ain't you're fucking drifting mate – Wake up and smell the format

**Jonathan** I can smell . . . engine fuel /

**Joe** Listen a' me yeah just listen to me. (*Beat.*) My dad.

**Jonathan** Yes.

**Joe** Now y'know my dad you met my dad Now my dad's a cunt but he's a useful cunt /

**Jonathan** Is he That's funny My dad's just a / cunt

**Joe** It's about property. (*Beat.*) Twenty years back he starts . . . dippin' the toe in Now, he's knee deep like you go Highbury . . . up the Angel all them parts there You look in any street, any street I bet there's more than one gaff there he's had suttin to do with like /

**Jonathan** See I didn't realise he's . . . a tycoon y'know I thought he was just . . . a plumber /

**Joe** The guy's got . . . shrewdness like . . . See that house there, my dad owns that shit. See that flat there, my dad put the carpets in that shit. See that house there, my dad bought the cunt off the council now he's muggin a load a' city boys five hundred a fucking week that's the way it goes *down* / like

**Jonathan** Oh that's the way it goes *down*, is / it

**Joe** People wanna live, where people wanna live.

**Jonathan** Course they do.

**Joe** And people own *things* and *things* are worth money and are kept in peoples houses Jonathan. (*Beat.*) Now I can get keys. That go in locks. (*Beat.*) And I can get codes. To all sorts of interesting things. (*Beat.*) Now. Are you on this, or are you on this?

  *Pause.*

**Jonathan** My dad's got a new flat.

  *Joe sighs.*

Yeah he's got a new . . . new lot a' things /

**Joe** Why am I wasting my time like I might as well ask your brother /

**Jonathan** When he, When he wakes up in the morning. (*Beat.*) Cup a' tea. (*Beat.*) Guardian. (*Beat.*) I'm, I'm sure . . . that his morning glory. Is made, that bit more . . . glorious. (*Beat.*) By the fact . . . By the knowledge. That his son, me, is safely minding the shop back home. (*Beat.*) Looking after Danny. Looking after me. (*Beat.*)

And most important of all, looking after my four, A levels. Four for the future. (*Beat.*) Now I want him, one day . . . to really wake up. And smell the format. (*Beat.*) So are you on this, or are you on this?

*Beat.*

**Joe** Well that's a nice idea then innit.

**Jonathan** It is very nice.

*Beat.*

**Joe** Sunday.

**Jonathan** Sunday /

**Lauren** (*singing, off*) See me in me pants and ting /

**Joe** Oh she finally shows / her ugly fucking face

*Lauren enters. She carries a retail-type uniform.*

**Lauren** (*singing, as she enters*) 'Them check say we hip and ting' /

**Joe** What you singing that / for (*To Jonathan.*) You see what I fucking have to deal with like I swear down

**Lauren** 'Love is all I bring . . . (*Kisses him.*) Inna me khaki suit and ting.' Oh my dizzy days Why you just screw up your face like that for? /

**Joe** I been stood here half an / hour

**Lauren** Oh /

**Joe** What you think I wanna sit about wi' this cunt waiting for you a' fucking / reach?

**Lauren** Oh baby shushy shushy it's coldy and my legs are hurty and I need a ciggy and I ain't got one in my / bag

**Joe** Oh well that's a shame for you /

31

**Lauren**  Come man /

**Joe**  Shall I give her that thing?

**Jonathan**  What? Yeah.

**Lauren**  What thing?

**Joe**  I don't think I wannoo now She's doing my brain / in

**Lauren**  Oh well you know how I feel then rude boy And who's *she*?

*Joe has produced an expensive-looking necklace.*

**Joe**  See it deh? Get on that. What you know about that That's moneys mate.

**Jonathan**  Yeah.

**Lauren**  Where you get dat?

**Joe**  What? 'Where you get dat . . . blood-clart ting / deh.'

*Lauren sighs.*

What's it matter wh– What's it matter where I fucking got it?

**Lauren**  You lift that out a' someone's suitcase now you want a Blue Peter badge /

**Joe**  Oh listen a' this cu– Next little yat'd be creamin her knickers over this You're giving it the *Crimewatch* routine

**Lauren**  Oh switch up the record I / beg you please Waste man.

**Joe**  For fu– Oi, Oi – You don't want it? – Suits me /

**Lauren**  You're in a mood, be in a mood like I don't care /

**Joe**  I'm going for a piss

**Lauren**  Well piss off then

**Joe** (*as he exits*) I am

**Lauren** Good

*She starts going through Joe's bag.*

**Lauren** Oh my word what a mish man.

**Jonathan** Yeah.

**Lauren** What a mush-clart mission and ting You want one a' these? (*Cigarette.*)

*Beat.*

**Jonathan** No.

*Pause.*

**Lauren** Don't you wish it was warm?

**Jonathan** Do you?

*Beat.*

**Lauren** Don't you wish it was 1987?

*Beat.*

**Jonathan** No. 'S bad enough as it is.

**Lauren** Is it.

*Beat.*

**Jonathan** I dunno Is it?

*Beat.*

**Lauren** How are you then Jonathan?

**Jonathan** Er, I'm . . . tired. Lauren. (*Beat.*) Er but I'm . . . alright.

**Lauren** Yeah?

*Beat.*

**Jonathan**  How are you?

*Beat.*

**Lauren**  Well if you're alright then I'm alright.

*Beat.*

**Jonathan**  Well that's alright then What's Joe like? These days?

**Lauren**  How you mean?

*Beat.*

**Jonathan**  Well I feel like I don't know him that good any more I dunno why.

*Beat.*

**Lauren**  Joe's Joe.

*Beat.*

**Jonathan**  Average.

*Beat. Joe re-enters, inspecting his trousers.*

**Joe**  'Ckin pissed down my trousers.

**Lauren**  That's nice.

**Joe**  (*to Lauren*) Come here.

*He kisses her.*

I'm a prick You know I'm a prick. What you doing today?

**Lauren**  Dunno. Come over if you want.

**Joe**  I'll come over you if you want.

*Lauren sucks her teeth.*

**Joe**  Don't f– . . . suck / your teeth at me

**Jonathan** I'm gonna make a move

**Joe** No we're all gonna make a move

**Lauren** You're giving me brain damage you / are

**Joe** Yeah you try spend the night in my fucking life I get a formal warning, for doing my job

**Jonathan** Yeah you wanna try . . .

*Joe exits.*

. . . spend the night in my life

**Lauren** Sun's coming up

**Joe** (*off*) Oh good I'll inform the media

**Lauren** Prick.

*Lauren puts her cigarette in Jonathan's mouth.*
*Blackout.*


## FOUR

*April.*
   *The dining room. Daniel is sitting with his eyes closed.*
*We can hear noise from the kitchen. Susan enters, with a*
*camera.*

**Susan** Right. Now.

**Daniel** Can I open them yet?

**Susan** Goodness me Where are we Yes. OK? Open up.

*Jonathan is bringing in a birthday cake with lighted*
*candles on it.*
   *Daniel opens his eyes.*
   *Beat.*

Oh, wow.

**Daniel**  Wow.

**Susan**  Well well well What a . . . fantastic . . . creation Well you know what to do don't you Danny.

**Daniel**  Are we, Are we gonna sing Happy Birthday again?

**Jonathan**  / No we're not.

**Susan**  No we won't sing it *again* sweetheart but I think those . . . rather nice . . . candles probably want . . . blowing out don't you?

**Jonathan**  (*to Susan*) Did you er . . .

**Susan**  (*to Daniel*) Don't you think?

**Daniel**  Yeah.

**Susan**  OK well off you go.

**Jonathan**  Did you get any . . . / message

**Susan**  Sssh.

   *Daniel tries to blow the candles out, but fails.*

(*Smiling.*) Oh . . .

**Daniel**  Sorry.

**Susan**  Try again. Try . . .

   *Daniel tries again. Blows some of them out.*

(*Clapping.*) Oh, well done.

**Daniel**  (*embarrassed*) Mum.

**Jonathan**  Just wondering if you got any message from Dad yet at all y'know / our father

**Susan**  Jonathan we have talked about this before I know you do enjoy /

**Daniel**  Mummy you / haven't taken a photo

**Jonathan**  What do I enjoy?

**Susan**  Yes I know I forgot I shall have to take the aftermath of the festivities Now move in chaps

**Daniel**  You're so forgetful some / times

**Jonathan**  Not as forgetful as . . . as some / people

**Susan**  Yes I know I am Jonathan move in please /

**Jonathan**  No I don't / wanna

**Daniel**  He doesn't want to be in / it

**Susan**  Well I'm sure he'll learn to . . . swallow / his pride

**Daniel**  I don't want him to be in / it

**Jonathan**  I feel . . . perfectly /

**Susan**  Just Just Just (*Mouths to him.*) Fucking move in.

    *Jonathan does so.*

There we are, now, pretend to be happy. (*Takes it.*) Very nice. Very nice.

**Daniel**  I actually made my Harry Potter face.

**Susan**  (*putting camera away*) Yes I saw that /

**Daniel**  'Cos if, 'Cos if I put my hair like that it makes . . . me look a bit like Harry Potter

**Susan**  Well I don't know about that Now do you want to see if Jonathan will show you what's in that bag?

**Daniel**  (*looking*) Well what . . . well what is in the bag?

**Jonathan**  Yeah what is in the bag?

**Susan**  You know what's in the bag.

**Jonathan**  What this bag?

**Susan** Jonathan.

*Beat. Jonathan starts unwrapping something out of a carrier bag.*

**Daniel** Is it ac– is it actually a surprise?

**Susan** Well . . .

*Beat.*

**Daniel** I love surprises. (*American accent.*) I just love surprises.

**Susan** I think this is something that Jonathan has . . . very specially . . .

*Jonathan produces a bottle of champagne.*

Ah. Now d'you know what that is Daniel?

**Daniel** Is it, is it alcohol?

**Susan** That is a bottle, of champagne.

**Daniel** Champagne?

**Susan** Sure is.

**Daniel** Well how much, well how much did that cost?

**Susan** Well it is a special treat and actually I didn't pay for it I think someone else paid for it didn't they.

**Jonathan** I didn't pay for it.

*Susan sighs.*

**Daniel** Well who, Well who did pay for it?

**Jonathan** I stole it.

**Daniel** You stole it?

**Susan** Jonathan is being . . . objectionable as usual /

**Jonathan** No, Jonathan is being very honest and and and unobjectionable

**Daniel**  / Bitch

**Susan**  Jonathan /

**Daniel**  Why did you steal it? /

**Susan**  He didn't steal it /

**Jonathan**  Well look Well as our father, who art in Dalston, once might have said, 'All property, is . . .' Well fuck it anyway Who's for Champers?

**Susan**  Yes, thank you Jonathan /

**Jonathan**  (*getting glasses*) Danny boy Birthday boy Birthday bloody . . . adult

**Daniel**  Can I, Can I try some? /

**Susan**  Yes well Jonathan's / just getting you some darling

**Jonathan**  (*opening bottle*) With your muggy little . . . Harry Potter bloody cap I tell you what you've had a result today

**Daniel**  Yeah I have /

**Jonathan**  I mean what d'you get like You got your . . .

**Daniel**  Well I got my Harry Potter / book

**Jonathan**  You got your Harry Potter book yeah

**Daniel**  I got my . . . I got my *Doctor Who* / DVD

**Jonathan**  You got your *Doctor Who* DVD yeah You got your Sugababes CD

**Daniel**  Yeah I love the Sugababes /

**Jonathan**  Yeah f– Who doesn't / like

**Susan**  This'll make a pop . . .

*Jonathan opens the bottle of champagne.*

There we are.

**Daniel**  It actually made quite a big noise.

**Susan**  Yes it did Thank you Jonathan.

**Daniel**  It actually, It actually sounded a bit like a fart

**Susan**  Yes well I think we hear quite enough of those already in this house thank you

**Daniel**  I don't /

**Jonathan**  (*distributing glasses*) But I tell you one – Here we go – I tell you one thing, that's really . . . There's just one thing, that's missing, don't you think Don't you get that / feeling

**Susan**  Well Cheers, anyway To the birthday boy /

**Daniel**  To me.

**Jonathan**  To absent friends. As they say.

*They all drink. Daniel grimaces.*

**Daniel**  Oh.

**Susan**  No?

*Beat.*

**Daniel**  It's actually . . .

**Susan**  Not . . . Not really . . .

**Daniel**  Not really no.

**Susan**  Well that's OK d'you want to / give –

**Jonathan**  Pass it I'll have it.

**Daniel**  No I don't want you to have it.

**Jonathan**  What?

**Daniel**  I don't want Jonathan to have it.

*Susan sighs.*

**Jonathan** Well chuck it down the sink then.

**Susan** No don't do that.

**Daniel** (*to Jonathan*) I can make my own decisions.

> *Beat.*

I'll put . . . I'll put it on the table there.

**Susan** Right.

**Daniel** (*to Jonathan*) But it's *not*, for you though.

**Susan** Danny why don't you get yourself a glass of water instead?

> *Beat.*

**Daniel** No I think I'd more . . . No I think I'd more prefer to have . . . some of my Easter egg.

**Susan** Well, Well you . . .

> *Daniel produces an Easter egg and starts eating.*

Because you've had some lovely presents today haven't you and that's –

> *Daniel hugs her.*

Oh, there we are, there we are. Now have you decided, between the pair of you, what you're going to do tomorrow?

**Daniel** (*sighs*) Well I'd much, rather, prefer . . . to do something with you, and not with Jonathan –

> *Jonathan laughs, softly.*

**Susan** Well darling I have to go back to work tomorrow because there are lots of little children who . . . who aren't as lucky as you and don't get to have a nice birthday like you and I have to go and . . . and help them.

**Daniel** Well Jonathan . . . creeps about like a creeper. And misses college.

**Susan** What on earth d'you mean? /

**Jonathan** What you talking about?

**Susan** Jonathan is there something you'd like to /

**Jonathan** What you t– I don't miss . . . college I never miss college

**Daniel** Well I know you do because I hear you, on the phone because . . . because you're gonna go and meet Joe because . . . because you're gonna go and meet Joe.

*Beat.*

**Susan** Well this is very interesting to know /

**Jonathan** Oh / f–

**Susan** because I . . . stupidly sort of thought that Joseph was . . . someone you would have the sense to be –

*Jonathan groans.*

– not hanging around with any more and as for /

**Jonathan** Well it would be interesting if it was true which it isn't /

**Susan** and as for . . . college I think you're three weeks away from your French . . . oral /

**Jonathan** Speaking te– It's not a fucking oral. It's a speaking te– It's not the fucking fifties /

**Daniel** Stop swearing you fucking bitch /

**Susan** Daniel will you please stop calling your brother a bitch?

**Daniel** Well he is one /

**Jonathan** (*reaching for champagne*) Gimme that bot–
I tell you what it's not going . . . very well . . . from your
point of view is it I mean the whole . . . happy families
thing like I mean I'm sorry but I just don't . . . buy it . . .
like I don't feel . . . hap– Do you feel happy– Danny
how's . . . Do you . . . feel /

**Susan** Jonathan sit down /

**Jonathan** I tell y– Where's . . . Dad It's a shame Da–
There's one thing . . . missing here It's a shame Daddy
couldn't be here isn't it /

**Daniel** Yeah, right He's more . . . He's more than worse
than you are /

**Susan** Jonathan he isn't . . . here and in a minute I'm
going to lose my temper /

**Jonathan** Oh g– I'll get the camera ready /

**Daniel** Shut up /

**Jonathan** He would have turned, to the birthday boy,
with his champagne glass in hand /

**Daniel** Get off!

*Daniel exits.*

**Jonathan** To his firstborn. (*Beat.*) I mean I know . . .
y'know he's doing his own thing but a Sm– a Smith's
token would a' done the trick wouldn't' it?

**Susan** One of these days, I think we're going to have a
very serious talk / about the way you behave

**Jonathan** (*fiddling with radio*) A serious ta– Yeah . . .
great when's, when's good for you like I mean I'm . . . I'm
here most days We might even catch him on the radio
like I'm sat in here the other day and he's on Radio 4,
talking about his book /

43

**Susan** Oh /

**Jonathan** Where you going? /

**Susan** I am going to talk to my f– to your brother, Jonathan, seeing as you've . . . driven a bulldozer through his birthday party /

**Jonathan** Well hold on I thought we were ha– I thought we were having a talk /

**Susan** (*off*) We will . . . talk Jonathan believe you me /

**Jonathan** Yeah f– Pencil me in. We'll . . . Get the diary out We'll t– We'll touch base. You fucking mug. (*Searching frequencies.*) Where is he?

*He searches through more frequencies.*

(*Shouting off.*) Mother? (*Beat.*) I can't find him.

*He settles on static. Swigs from his drink. Beat.*

I c– . . . (*Beat.*) I can't find him.

*Blackout. In the blackout, the radio static dissolves into an excerpt from a radio interview with Sean;*

**Sean** – and I think what's interesting is that the influence of the . . . the archetypes of say the fifties and the sixties has become . . . detectable on a broader . . . spectrum of cultural / analysis

**Voice** And this is broadly the point which is made in the book is it not? /

**Sean** It is, It is the . . .

**Voice** The longevity of /

**Sean** The longevity of, of this iconography which is quite . . . assured . . .

44

## FIVE

*May.*
   *Jonathan and Joe, in someone's flat in Islington. Night. A small suitcase is on the floor in front of them.*

**Joe** Who's shouting?

**Jonathan** It's /

**Joe** I'm not shouting who's shouting?!

**Jonathan** You're f– What was that?

**Joe** (*laughs*) Nothing is what / it was –

**Jonathan** I heard, something /

**Joe** Oh go home. You soppy prick Go sit on the sofa wi' your dick in your right / hand

**Jonathan** We have to think about / this

**Joe** 'We have to think about this.' Get your pinny on you fucking woman

**Jonathan** (*indicating suitcase*) Open it again

**Joe** You open it again.

   *Beat.*

**Jonathan** Who lives here?

**Joe** How am I suppos– I dunno some geezer.

**Jonathan** What you know him you met you / what?

**Joe** Course I don't know him I wouldn't know him if he rubbed me up the bum /

**Jonathan** (*sighs*) Oh this is bad, This is bad /

**Joe** Jonathan this is a *touch* like /

**Jonathan**  There's about fifty grams a' coke in here

**Joe**  Oh so you did notice.

*Beat*

**Jonathan**  Who walks about with fifty grams a' coke on 'em?

**Joe**  Well he doesn't he keeps 'em under the bed

**Jonathan**  Maybe he's . . . a gangster

**Joe**  Fucki– Maybe he runs Channel 4 John /

**Jonathan**  What do you know, about this guy? /

**Joe**  What do *I* know about him I know he lives in a nice big flat for a grand a week I know his burglar alarm code is eighteen-ninety-six I know . . . (*Picking up receipt.*) He goes to Carluccio's in Upper Street What are we getting wet about like /

*Jonathan sighs.*

All you had to do, was climb over a few walls, watch a few windows and now, here comes the jackpot /

**Jonathan**  Yeah a few . . . iPods and a telly's one thing /

**Joe**  What you want me to put it back? What like What we gonna do?

**Jonathan**  F– . . . About twenty years . . .

*Joe sucks his teeth.*

**Jonathan**  . . . I reckon wi' that lot Look . . . Empathy Look at this from my point a' view right /

*Joe groans.*

Tomorrow morning I'm sat in that sports hall yeah I'm sitting A level English Joe /

46

**Joe** Yeah let's, let's look at it from your point a' view for a change like Let's think about the future. (*Beat.*) Y'know. (*Beat.*) For a minute. (*Beat.*) Y'know twenty years' time you come home . . . got your little . . . office job . . . qualifications all them . . . things there like /

**Jonathan** I don't wanna talk / about this

**Joe** There's a knock at the door the middle a' the night there's a knock on the bedroom door. Who is it. (*Beat.*) Oh fuck me it's Danny John. It's Danny. (*Beat.*) You . . . What you think he's gone away? Yeah? Think someone's . . . took him out the frame for you They ain't, They haven't He's still, fucking, there And maybe . . . it's a real cunt, that you've gotta get up, and change his pissy sheets for him in the middle a' the night again and again 'cos that's the way it's gonna go down mate /

**Jonathan** Please . . . Do me a / favour

**Joe** (*indicating suitcase*) 'Cos life throws up a whole heap a' madness right and if you can't roll with it, get rolled over /

**Jonathan** (*half-laughs*) Roll– . . .

   *Beat.*

**Joe** So what.

   *Pause.*

**Jonathan** Who's gonna sort us out?

   *Beat.*

**Joe** Alexei.

**Jonathan** Oh God.

**Joe** What's the matter wi' you like the guy's connected /

**Jonathan** And he's a fucking lunatic /

**Joe** Or scratch that You could do it school.

**Jonathan** What?

**Joe** All them little neekos down there fuckin . . . hangin out for a bit naughtiness like I bet you could do all that in a week.

**Jonathan** This is the last one.

   *Beat.*

**Joe** Course it is. (*Beat.*) No more . . . creeping and . . . codes and . . . other people's back doors like after this we make moves like we progress.

**Jonathan** Maybe you do I don't.

**Joe** What?

**Jonathan** I said maybe you do. (*Beat.*) I've, I've got . . . People are . . .

   *Beat.*

**Joe** Come on let's bounce. Get an early night for your little exam.

   *Beat.*

**Jonathan** Alexei . . . I mean he'll probably try and . . . boy us out of it anyway /

**Joe** Yeah then I'll punch him all over the gaff.

**Jonathan** We smash a window on the way out.

**Joe** What? Why?

   *Beat.*

**Jonathan** To make it look more . . . opportunistic.

   *Beat. Joe starts laughing. Jonathan laughs back.*

**Joe** (*exiting*) You said it bruv.

**Jonathan** (*stops laughing*) Yeah.

*Blackout. In the blackout, we hear a bit of a scene from a Harry Potter DVD.*


SIX

*June.*
  *The living room at Jonathan's house. It's the middle of a warm night – the windows are open. The TV is on quietly – a Harry Potter DVD is playing. Daniel is watching it intently. He is joining in with Harry Potter's dialogue.*

**Daniel** 'I'm a what?'

. . .

'No. You've made a mistake I mean . . . I . . . can't be a . . . a wizard. I mean I'm . . . just . . . Harry. Just Harry.'

*Beat. Daniel notices that Jonathan has entered, half-asleep. Daniel quickly turns the DVD off. Beat. Jonathan sighs.*

**Jonathan** I've changed the sheets on the bed Come . . . Get in the bed now . . . Danny go back to bed.

*Pause.*

Daniel. (*Beat.*) I've got an exam tomorrow.

*Pause.*

Look I know, it's hot. (*Beat.*) I'm hot. (*Beat.*) The window's are . . . I've opened the wi– Why you wearing shoes? (*Beat.*) What have you got your shoes on for? (*Beat.*) Daniel /

**Daniel** Shut up. (*Beat.*) I'm leaving.

*Beat.*

**Jonathan** What?

**Daniel** You heard. (*Beat.*) One d–, One d– . . . One d– . . . One d– /

**Jonathan** 'One d– One d–' What?

*Beat.*

**Daniel** One day, I'm going to go away, and never come back.

**Jonathan** Oh f– . . . Good yeah good Do, Do us all a favour /

**Daniel** Why, are you always, not here? (*Beat.*) Because . . . Because you're supposed to be here.

*Jonathan stares at him, exasperated. Pause.*

Where's Mum?

**Jonathan** (*sighs*) She had to go to work She's on call.

*Beat.*

**Daniel** Well Mum says, that you've been spending too much time, with Joe.

*Beat.*

**Jonathan** Oh she says that does she?

**Daniel** Yeah she does.

**Jonathan** Well I'm pleased for her.

**Daniel** Go away.

*Pause.*

**Jonathan** No.

*Pause.*

**Daniel** I want to go on the balcony.

**Jonathan** You go on the balcony then.

*Beat. Daniel moves slowly towards the exit, then stops. Pause.*

**Daniel** Can you do my laces up please?

**Jonathan** What?

**Daniel** Can you do my laces up.

*Pause.*

**Jonathan** Yeah.

*Jonathan kneels down and starts tying Daniel's shoelaces, slowly. He finishes the first one, then stops. Pause.*

**Daniel** Well what– . . . Well what is it?

*Pause. Jonathan looks up at him.*

**Jonathan** Tell me what to do, because I dunno what to do any more.

*Beat.*

Daniel.

**Daniel** Leave me alone.

*Daniel exits. Pause. Blackout.*

*In the blackout, Lauren enters and starts sorting through a box of vinyl records. A door buzzer goes – she gets up and goes to answer it.*

## SEVEN

*July.*
  *The living room at Joe's house. Lauren enters and paces. Beat.*

**Jonathan** (*off*) Yeah yeah yeah /

**Lauren** I'm in here.

**Jonathan** (*off*) You're in there. Woy . . . I'm in here
You're in there /

**Lauren** I'm . . . flu'd out y'know I might . . .

  *Jonathan enters, a bit coked up and carrying the
  suitcase from before.*

. . . breathe 'pon you and spread that shit.

**Jonathan** Yeah? So it's you.

  *Beat.*

**Lauren** Yeah it is me yeah /

**Jonathan** Yeah it is you yeah it's . . . I didn't expect you
to be here like /

**Lauren** No? /

**Jonathan** I was expecting . . . Joe but . . .

**Lauren** Surprises.

**Jonathan** Surprises.

  *Beat.*

**Lauren** Come nice innit, when you don't expect them.

**Jonathan** They do. They do. (*Beat.*) What you moving in
with him now or suttin /

**Lauren**  Shut up man I'm just passin tru like /

**Jonathan**  You're just passin tru, though, you get me though /

**Lauren**  What you going on with / like?

**Jonathan**  Yeah so am I I'm just . . .

**Lauren**  What's in the thing?

*Jonathan looks at the suitcase.*

**Jonathan**  The thing? Errr . . .

*Beat.*

**Lauren**  You want a drink?

*Beat.*

**Jonathan**  A dr– . . .

*Beat.*

**Lauren**  Y'know a drink. (*Beat.*) To drink.

*Beat.*

**Jonathan**  Er. Well. Funny you should say that because, Yes. Please. I would. Please. Thank you.

**Lauren**  OK.

**Jonathan**  Where's Joe?

**Lauren**  (*off*) I dunno I don't care.

**Jonathan**  (*half-laughs*) Yeah.

**Lauren**  (*re-entering with drinks*) Y'know he'll be . . . creepin' about somewhere the lickle rarse.

**Jonathan**  It's fucking – ta – It's hot weather innit like.

**Lauren**  Yeah.

**Jonathan** Anyone'd think it was . . . summer. Y'know. And they'd be right. (*Suitcase.*) Oh yeah I was gonna leave this here for him, erm /

**Lauren** You can do I won't look.

**Jonathan** Erm . . .

**Lauren** (*indicating records*) You see how much shit they got in here man This is some . . . old-skool . . . lick-shots / like

**Jonathan** (*laughs*) Lick-shots Yeah the boy's, he's /

**Lauren** Oh my / word

**Jonathan** full a' secrets like

**Lauren** Louisa Marks 1979 My *Mum*'s too young for this And you know what?

**Jonathan** What?

**Lauren** Last week or some rubbishness he tells me he's got a cousin, at LAM records

   *Beat.*

**Jonathan** Wow that's . . . that's deep that's . . . What's that mean?

**Lauren** Studio time man that's what that means.

**Jonathan** Oh yeah yeah /

**Lauren** You think I wanna be stuck in some . . . foolish little retail job all my life You mad?

**Jonathan** Why d'you listen to all this . . . old stuff like eighties and and and Don't you think that says suttin about you though. (*Beat.*) Lauren.

   *Beat.*

**Lauren** What's it say about me?

**Jonathan** F– I wouldn't like to say like I wouldn't . . . (*Beat.*) I tell you what I'm sweating like.

**Lauren** Yeah tell me about it /

**Jonathan** I don't wanna tell you about it. To be honest. It's . . . disgusting out here y'know it's . . .

**Lauren** Are you buzzin?

   *Beat.*

**Jonathan** What? No. What you t– . . .

   *Lauren laughs, softly. Jonathan laughs back.*

I'm on a . . . bit a' . . .

**Lauren** You can have some Lemsip if you want.

   *Beat.*

**Jonathan** Yeah?

**Lauren** 'S up to you.

   *Beat.*

**Jonathan** Well I'm . . . Yeah I'm . . . quite . . . getting a . . .

   *Beat. Jonathan blows air out of his mouth. Beat.*

So you're wearing a dressing gown then.

**Lauren** I am yeah.

**Jonathan** Well that's . . . it's a lovely day for it.

**Lauren** For what?

**Jonathan** Anything Are you sick?

**Lauren** What?

**Jonathan** Are you ill?

**Lauren** Yeah I told you man I got flu.

**Jonathan** Flu.

**Lauren** That's what I said.

*Pause.*

**Jonathan** Y'know some . . . people like they *say* . . . that they're *ill*, like.

*Pause.*

**Lauren** Yeah?

*Pause.*

**Jonathan** But the reality is that *they're* . . . not, *ill,* as *such*.

*Beat.*

They're le*thar*gic.

*Beat.*

**Lauren** Is that right.

**Jonathan** I think it is. (*Beat.*) I think i– Not that I'm . . . tryin' a' say . . . something *bad* like not that . . . certain people . . . I need some water like I got . . . I got some water in my bag /

**Lauren** Did you try to ring me last night?

*Jonathan chokes on his water. Beat.*

**Jonathan** Come again?

*Lauren gets her phone out.*

**Lauren** Yeah I get a missed call from . . . Jonathan mob. (*Beat.*) Maybe it went off in your pocket.

*Pause. Jonathan half-laughs.*

**Jonathan** Erm. Yeah I was at p– a party last night d'you know, d'you know Jason . . . Phillips?

**Lauren** Nope.

**Jonathan** Yeah me and him and . . . and Joe and . . .
(*Indicating window.*) We used to go a' that primary
school.

**Lauren** Yeah I know Jonathan.

**Jonathan** Well not . . . I mean I joined in /

**Lauren** I used to go there too.

　*Beat.*

**Jonathan** Oh yeah course you did course you did /

**Lauren** Course I did. I been here. (*Beat.*) Always.

　*Pause.*

**Jonathan** I remember watching you in the Year Six play.

**Lauren** Yeah?

　*Beat.*

**Jonathan** Yeah I thought you were very good. Very good.
(*Beat.*) Always quite fancied you a bit to be hon–
Anyway I'll put this on the er . . . (*His drink.*) I'll put this
on the . . .

**Lauren** The table?

　*Beat.*

**Jonathan** Yeah. Yeah yeah. (*Beat.*) 'The table.'

　*Pause.*

Er . . . So we had our last . . . exam on . . . Tuesday
and . . . So there was this party . . . last night but I'm . . .
stood there in the . . . crowd and . . . and I'm looking
around and y'know, y'know, y'know, y'know you . . . look
a . . . round and . . . all the faces and . . . you think . . .

*Pause.*

So I thought I'll call . . . I had to call . . . someone and . . .

*Pause.*

So there you go.

*Pause.*

**Lauren** Are you happy then?

*Beat.*

**Jonathan** What? /

**Lauren** Are you happy you must be . . . happy.

*Jonathan hesitates. Beat.*

Well I'm . . . would be if I was you. Got your . . . exams all done. Future . . . all . . .

**Jonathan** (*half-laughs*) Well I'm . . .

*Pause. Jonathan indicates the suitcase.*

Have a look inside.

*Beat.*

**Lauren** Thought it's for Joe.

*Beat.*

**Jonathan** Well he's not in is he.

*Beat. Lauren opens the suitcase and pulls out a gram of coke. Beat.*

**Lauren** You just keep coming wi' them little surprises don't you Jonathan.

**Jonathan** Do I. (*Beat.*) Joe can have it I don't want it. Tell him I don't wanna keep things for him, at my place any more my mum'll find 'em my . . . brother nearly found it a . . . the other day Tell him, he's on his own.

*Beat.*

**Lauren** I / don't

**Jonathan** (*indicating coke*) You ever done . . .

*Lauren shakes her head.*

Neither had I. Y'see. I hadn't even . . . That party like
I swear like people . . . cheered . . . when, when I walked
in like I'm getting a reputa– I never had . . . one a' them /
before

**Lauren** Jon– Jonathan, Joe . . . will be angry. (*Beat.*) If
you fuck him about.

*Beat.*

**Jonathan** Yeah he's . . . My, My mum says he's like a
time bomb. Waiting to go off I thought that was quite
good . . . by her / standards

**Lauren** (*laughs*) Jonathan /

**Jonathan** I thought that was quite astute. As they say /

**Lauren** You need to slow down.

**Jonathan** Can you feel that?

**Lauren** Feel what?

*Beat.*

**Jonathan** Your heart's beating.

**Lauren** It does that yeah.

*Beat.*

**Jonathan** But anyway I don't wanna do that any more
I don't wanna sell, or buy. Tell . . . tell Joe to stop ringing
me to see if I wanna do things 'cos I don't wanna do
things I don't wanna do . . . anything any more I . . .
All . . .

**Lauren**  Well what do you wanna do /

**Jonathan**  All my brother wants, is a garden. (*Beat.*) But we haven't got one, we haven't. We haven't got one.

**Lauren**  Come here.

*He puts her hand on his chest.*

**Jonathan**  Can you feel that? What you doing tonight?

**Lauren**  Who's asking?

**Jonathan**  I'm asking Look I know . . . I'm buzzin, and . . . I talk a load a' shit and . . . my brother's /

**Lauren**  Shut up a minute /

**Jonathan**  But I've always liked your hands.

*Beat. He laughs. She laughs back.*

**Lauren**  Yeah?

**Jonathan**  No, I mean . . . You've got fucking great . . . hands I've always . . . (*Takes her hand.*) Your dad . . . was black wasn't he I remember . . . Always thought you had the most incredible . . . fingers /

**Lauren**  Shhh.

*He rests his forehead on hers. They kiss. Pause.*

**Jonathan**  (*softly*) I'm alright now. (*Beat.*) I'm alright now.

*He holds her hand up to the light. Beat. He puts her hand on his chest, over his heart. Blackout.*

## EIGHT

*August.*
*Rain. A shelter in a park. Night. Jonathan and Joe.*
*Both are wet from the rain. Joe's face and hand is*
*severely bruised. Pause.*

**Joe** You been away then.

*Beat.*

**Jonathan** No.

*Beat.*

**Joe** You been hiding somewhere /

**Jonathan** I been round here 's been alright. 'S been good.

*Beat.*

**Joe** Oh well that's good.

**Jonathan** Yeah. (*Beat.*) I never used to like the summer.

*Beat.*

Joe How's your brother?

*Beat.*

**Jonathan** Same as. / Getting worse. (*Beat.*)

*Beat.*

Got my A levels.

**Joe** Yeah?

**Jonathan** Yeah not good not good. (*Beat.*) Who cares.

*Pause.*

**Joe** I got a few things I wanna talk about.

*Beat.*

**Jonathan** We used to come to this park didn't we all the time. Why don't we come to this park any more?

**Joe** Because it's shit.

   *Pause.*

**Jonathan** What's the matter wi' your face?

**Joe** What's the matter with your brain? (*Beat.*) 'Cos you're going on stupid Jonathan innit What you playing at You don't blank *me*. On the phone. On the text. When I try a' ring you What you going on with like I'm not some sort a' / prick

**Jonathan** I lost my phone.

**Joe** Oh yeah?

**Jonathan** Yeah. (*Beat.*) Then I found it.

   *Joe paces. Jonathan watches him. Pause. He starts laughing.*

**Joe** I f– . . . What you laughing at?

**Jonathan** Just . . .

**Joe** What?

**Jonathan** I just find you a bit funny.

**Joe** Fu– Oh bit funny?

**Jonathan** Yeah bit / amusing

**Joe** Bit funny Oh yeah I f– . . . I could do with a laugh

**Jonathan** I mean how long have I known you like I know you from we were this tall. (*Beat.*) And in those days . . . (*Beat.*) Y'know I mean things move on don't they things / move

**Joe** Stop talking you little dick.

*Beat.*

**Jonathan** But yeah I look at you now. (*Beat.*) Like I'm doing. (*Beat.*) It's funny You look like a child to me. (*Beat.*) I mean it's a compliment it's a c– . . . Don't get me wrong y'know it's . . . (*Beat.*) Still six years old to me. (*Beat.*) All the years.

*Pause. Joe examines his fist. He shows Jonathan the scar on it.*

**Joe** See that. Look a' that.

*Joe punches him in the face.*

**Jonathan** (*clutching his nose, whispering*) Fuck, fuck.

*Jonathan moves away. Beat.*

**Joe** John. John. (*Beat.*) There's plenty more where that come from. Y'understand? Yeah?

*Jonathan nods.*

Now what's going on? (*Beat.*) Ha?

**Jonathan** (*half-laughs*) I w– . . . I wish I knew Joe boy /

**Joe** Don't f–, Don't fucking boy me off you cunt I'll bang you out

**Jonathan** Joe /

**Joe** I'll fucking kill you

**Jonathan** Joe /

**Joe** Look at me. (*Indicates his bruised face.*) Yeah? (*Beat.*) Well let me tell you what's been happening

**Jonathan** Joe /

**Joe** Don't fucking 'Joe' me cunt I'll bang you spark out Now I'm on the phone, to Danny Milton right remember him? (*Beat.*) Now he's put it about that there's a nice little flat worth a look, over by Clissold yeah? Now I'm thinking 'Yes this is a bit a' me like This is moneys still,' but what's happened to Jonathan? (*Beat.*) Y'know he ain't on the phone, he ain't on the text Guy's– . . . He's away wi' the fucking fairies in' he Well fuck him. I'll do it on the ones. (*Beat.*) So I've rolled up there Jonathan. And I, I can't carry too much . . . on my own y'know which is a bit of a fucker But I'm just luggin this . . . DVD player down the . . . hallway when I he– suddenly I hear this . . . noise this . . . toilet-flushing noise . . . behind me I turn around and this . . . big old geezer is coming out the bathroom door, trousers round his fucking legs and I'm running . . .

*Beat. He half-laughs.*

You can only run so far though can't you John boy. (*Beat.*) I can barely fucking see out a' this one but y'know That's what happens, when you get boyed off by your best mate, and left to do your runnings on your own /

**Jonathan** I told you . . . I wasn't gonna do it any more. (*Beat.*) So I don't.

*Pause.*

**Joe** Oh well that's it then is it?

**Jonathan** I don't know I hope so. I hope so for you /

**Joe** The amount a' times I've had to bail your . . . skinny little arse out of / it

**Jonathan** 'Cos you're only gonna get yourself . . .

**Joe** What? What? Rich? (*Beat.*) Happy? (*Beat.*) Contented? /

**Jonathan** I don't think so. I don't.

*Beat.*

**Joe** Well that ain't my / problem

**Jonathan** I think you're gonna get yourself . . .
disappointed. (*Beat.*) And lonely. (*Beat.*) End up . . .
somewhere . . . you can't come back from.

   *Pause.*

I'm s– . . . (*Beat.*) I'm sorry . . . for . . .

   *Pause.*

**Joe** Where is she then?

   *Beat.*

**Jonathan** What?

**Joe** Where is she? (*Beat.*) Tonight.

   *Beat.*

**Jonathan** Where's . . . Who's /

**Joe** (*half-laughs*) Don't take the piss out' a me. (*Beat.*)
I saw you. (*Beat.*) I saw the pair a' ya. Saturday night.

   *Pause.*

**Jonathan** She said you er . . . (*Beat.*) Said you said . . .
you were gonna get her some . . . time. In a studio. Some
studio time. (*Beat.*) But you never did. (*Beat.*) Said you
were gonna . . . fix yourself up. Properly. (*Beat.*) But you
never did.

**Joe** Where's she staying? I been round her mum's she
ain't there. What she, she plotted up wi' you now?

**Jonathan** No.

**Joe** Where's she staying?

   *Beat.*

**Jonathan** She went to the carnival / today

**Joe**  I ain't gonna fucking ask you / again

**Jonathan**  Ask what /

*Joe hits him again. He kicks him. Pause.*

Don't . . . Don't you feel quite . . . privileged? (*Beat.*) To be here now.

*Joe laughs, shaking his head.*

To be young, and here, and alive. (*Beat.*) Not many people can say that.

**Joe**  Oh well that's all nice then innit how nice. Nice to wake up in the morning and think y'know There is something. For me. (*Beat.*) Y'know There is, something Well what is there? For me. (*Beat.*) D'you get my meaning? (*Beat.*) D'you understand, what I'm talking about? /

**Jonathan**  No I don't . . . quite understand you Joe /

*Joe hits him again.*

D'you think . . . D'you think you could give me suttin in writing?

*Pause.*

**Joe**  I'm gonna make you wish you never met me.

*Joe exits. Beat.*

**Jonathan**  Bye Joe See you Joe. See you tomorrow Joe see you at school. (*Beat.*) Yeah what you got . . . first lesson what's . . . What day is it we'll go up town . . . after school We'll go Trocadero. (*Beat.*) Yeah I see you then Joe. (*Beat.*) Nice one Joe boy.

*Pause. Blackout.*

## NINE

*September.*
    *The living room at Jonathan's house. Susan is sitting down, looking at some photos. Pause. The sound of keys in a lock. She looks towards the door. Lauren enters, unexpectedly. She has earphones in – she's singing 'Bridges and Balloons' by Joanna Newsom.*

**Lauren** (*singing*) 'But ships are fallible I say, and the na –'

    *They look at each other. Beat.*

Oh. (*Beat.*) Hello.

**Susan** Hello.

**Lauren** (*laughs*) Hi you must be Susan.

**Susan** Yes I suppose I must be.

**Lauren** Hi I'm . . . Lauren.

**Susan** Hello Lauren how nice to meet you.

**Lauren** Nice to meet / you too

**Susan** You must /

**Lauren** I was only erm . . .

**Susan** You must be Jonathan's . . .

    *Beat.*

**Lauren** Er yeah I am . . . Jonathan's . . .

**Susan** Well how good to finally m– I mean he's told me so much . . . Well what am I talking about actually he's told me very little about you . . .

**Lauren** Oh /

**Susan** As with everything else . . . in his life /

67

**Lauren**  Oh there's nothing to say

**Susan**  Oh don't be / silly

**Lauren**  No / the –

**Susan**  There's always . . .

**Lauren**  No there isn't. There really isn't.

**Susan**  Modesty.

   *Beat.*

**Lauren**  I sh– /

**Susan**  Would you like a cup of tea?

**Lauren**  Er Well I just really come to er . . . Yeah. Yes
please.

**Susan**  (*exiting*) Excellent You've come just in time.

**Lauren**  (*half-laughs*) Yeah I let myself . . . Jonathan left
his . . . keys behind /

**Susan**  (*off*) Yes that sounds like Jonathan.

**Lauren**  (*producing a pair of boxer shorts from her bag*)
And some other . . . things /

**Susan**  (*re-entering*) You don't take sugar or anything like
that do you Lauren?

   *Beat.*

**Lauren**  Er . . . I don't have to.

**Susan**  Ah but do you want to?

**Lauren**  Er . . . Yeah, / yeah please if you've got

**Susan**  In fact no yes of course, of course you want some.
Of course you do So do I. We shall both . . . there we are.

**Lauren**  Thanks.

**Susan** Jonathan has gone to . . . a careers fair.

**Lauren** Oh yeah I thought he / was

**Susan** To go and look for a career Would you like some fruit?

**Lauren** Oh no I'm . . .

   *Beat.*

It's funny weather isn't it.

**Susan** Yes it is rather.

**Lauren** Dunno whether it's autumn or summer or . . .

**Susan** Yes.

   *Beat.*

**Lauren** Well. (*Beat.*) Be Christmas soon. (*Beat.*) I start thinking about . . . Christmas . . . soon as the summer's over /

**Susan** D'you really?

**Lauren** Yeah it's . . . sad.

   *Beat.*

**Susan** Well October's . . . something to look forward to isn't it? Leaves?

**Lauren** Yeah I suppose. (*Tea.*) This is nice. This is lovely.

   *Beat.*

**Susan** How old are you Lauren?

**Lauren** Eighteen. How old are you?

**Susan** (*half-laughs*) I'm, fifty-two. (*Nods.*) Fifty-two.

**Lauren** That's a good age.

**Susan** D'you think so?

**Lauren** I think so yeah you must know . . . what's what.

*Beat.*

**Susan** Well I'd rather be eightee– Well I'm not sure I would rather be . . . eighteen actually Where did I put my . . . / (*spoon*)?

**Lauren** So you must've enjoyed . . . the eighties then?

**Susan** Enjoyed the / eighties

**Lauren** Well you must remember them anyway.

**Susan** Yes I do remember the eighties they were . . . all the rage for a time /

**Lauren** Yeah I'm . . . into . . . I sing.

**Susan** Oh I see. (*Beat.*) I don't.

**Lauren** That's alright. Neither can Jonathan.

**Susan** Did you, go to college . . . with /

**Lauren** Oh no I never went . . . college /

**Susan** Oh well that's a shame Why ever not? You're a . . . bright girl?

**Lauren** So? (*Beat.*) I didn't want to.

*Beat.*

**Susan** Yes. Yes well that's . . .

**Lauren** I worked at the airport.

**Susan** Oh so that's where / you

**Lauren** Well it was Jonathan's idea to . . . for the three of us like But I knew him already from . . . (*Beat.*) Anyway John . . . jacked that in same time as I did.

**Susan** Did he really?

*Beat.*

**Lauren**  Didn't you know?

*Beat.*

**Susan**  Er, no. No well that makes a lot of sense.

**Lauren**  Yeah he's a bit . . . mad like that.

**Susan**  Yes.

*Pause.*

This is er . . . This is a letter. For Jonathan. From the University of . . . North-East London.

**Lauren**  Oh, oh yeah?

**Susan**  Which is the only . . . institution that has offered him a place . . .

**Lauren**  Oh well that's . . .

**Susan**  . . . due to his rather . . . disappointing . . . A level results.

*Beat.*

**Lauren**  Yeah. (*Beat.*) That's . . .

**Susan**  Lauren I wonder if . . . (*Half-laughs. Beat.*) D'you think you could tell me what's happened to Jonathan?

*Beat. Lauren half-laughs.*

You obviously seem to know him a bit better than I do . . . at the moment because I, I, I seem . . . to know him . . . hardly at all. (*Beat.*) Any more. (*Beat.*) We've had our . . . ups and downs but even . . . He still . . . talked to me still . . . looked at me. Without contempt. (*Beat.*) And he worked, hard We should all . . .

*Pause.*

**Lauren** I hated school. (*Half-laughs.*) I went to about five schools. (*Beat.*) When I was thirteen, I ran away. (*Beat.*) I came back.

*Pause.*

**Susan** For my . . . job I, have to . . .

**Lauren** What do you do?

**Susan** Well I work for social se– I'm a social worker.

**Lauren** Oh.

**Susan** In Waltham Forest. So it takes me to . . . a lot of families I must say My job is to . . . help them. (*Beat.*) To help themselves.

*Daniel has entered. He is silent – sulking. He looks at them. Beat.*

Hello sweetheart this is Lauren.

**Lauren** Hi.

*Daniel picks up a CD and some headphones, then exits. Beat.*

**Susan** Have you met Daniel before?

**Lauren** Er yeah I've . . .

**Susan** He's being . . . rather difficult at the moment as you can . . .

**Lauren** (*laughs*) Yeah he's /

**Susan** When he was . . . younger we could . . . move him from . . . special school to . . . mainstream school to . . . arts college to . . . residential schools in in . . . Hackney and Leicester and St Albans and Birmingham and all this of course was hugely beneficial to his . . . But now, he is . . . twenty-five and is . . . discouraged from attending . . . the youth club because, he is not . . . a youth he is . . . an adult and the council gives us a huge amount of money but doesn't seem to have the faintest idea what they want us to do with it Does Jonathan talk . . . about Daniel?

*Beat.*

**Lauren** He . . . (*Beat.*) Sometimes, I think he gets . . . frustrated.

**Susan** (*laughs*) Sometimes I think he'd rather he . . . crawled up and died, somewhere. (*Beat.*) Like an animal. (*Beat.*) Certainly I . . . (*Beat.*) Certainly his father . . .

**Lauren** I think Jonathan needs . . .

*Beat.*

**Susan** Well anyway enough ab– What about you, What about your . . . D'you like . . . your . . . family?

**Lauren** Well. (*Beat.*) My dad's not around. Prick.

*They smile.*

My mum's . . . OK yeah she's . . . (*Half-laughs.*) she's good.

**Susan** Good.

**Lauren** I put my little sister in hospital once. This is years ago I . . . smacked her head against a . . . wall That's . . . that's families.

*Beat.*

**Susan** You . . . you said you . . . sing, you /

**Lauren** Er, I sing yeah. I try.

*Beat.*

**Susan** D'you think you might . . . sing something now?

*Beat.*

**Lauren**  Now?

**Susan**  You don't have to.

*Beat.*

**Lauren**  What . . . (*Half-laughs.*) . . . d'you wanna hear?

**Susan**  Anything you like.

*Pause. Lauren laughs.*

**Lauren**  Well.

*Pause. She starts singing – '99 Red Balloons'.
Tentative at first, but gaining in confidence.*

'You and I, in a little toy shop,
Buy a bag of balloons with the money we've got.
Set them free, at the break of dawn,
Till one by one, they were gone.

'Back at base, ssssomething the software,
Flash the message, something's out there.
Floating in the summer sky,
Ninety-nine red balloons go / by.'

*A phone starts ringing, off. Susan lets it ring off.
Pause.*

**Susan**  Well that was lovely thank / you very much

**Lauren**  Oh it was . . . (*Beat.*) I'm bad I'm bad. I'm too bad.

**Susan**  Well if you really thought that then you wouldn't do it would you.

*Beat.*

**Lauren**  No I, suppose not.

*Pause.*

**Susan**  Will you tell . . . Jonathan . . . that I'm . . .

74

*Pause. Lauren smiles, nods. Beat.*

(*Sighs, smiling.*) That I'm . . . a silly old woman. But he knows that I'm sure.

**Lauren** This . . . used to be all . . . fields. Once. (*Beat.*) All round here. Long time ago. (*Beat.*) All fields and . . . open.

*Pause.*

**Susan** Yes.

*Pause.*

**Lauren** Well that's gotta be something. (*Beat.*) Hasn't it.

*Pause. Blackout.*


## TEN

*October.*
    *Joe and Daniel, in the corner of a pub. Joe is watching Daniel slowly drinking a JD's and Coke.*

**Joe** That's it. (*Beat.*) Aaah that's it that's the one.

    *Daniel finishes the drink, smiling.*

Rah. (*Beat.*) Yeah?

**Daniel** I ac– I actually really like it.

**Joe** Yeah well you like Coke . . .

**Daniel** Yeah I do.

**Joe** Yeah well you like . . . Jack Daniel's bloody . . . as well now

**Daniel** Yeah I do /

**Joe** Yeah you do you want another one?

**Daniel**  Another one?

**Joe**  Yeah why not man?

**Daniel**  Yeah I w– Yeah I w– Yeah I w– Yeah I w– Yeah I would actually quite like one /

**Joe**  (*spilling small change onto table*) Course you would now let's see what we got here like /

**Daniel**  Are you . . . actually going to go . . . trick or treating tonight?

    *Beat.*

**Joe**  What? Oh no I ain't . . .

**Daniel**  Me neither.

**Joe**  Nah that's some . . . batty hole thing innit

**Daniel**  Yeah.

    *Beat.*

**Joe**  (*money*) I don't think I got . . . enough . . .

**Daniel**  Thanks for a good time today.

    *Beat.*

**Joe**  What?

**Daniel**  I mean it.

**Joe**  Yeah we only . . .

**Daniel**  I've actually had a not a good a time as . . . as today as . . . hardly ever.

**Joe**  (*half-laughs*) Wow. (*Beat.*) No me neither.

    *Beat.*

**Daniel**  Is there a toilet here?

**Joe**  What? Oh yeah yeah it's . . .

*Joe watches him stand up. Beat.*

You don't need me a' . . .

**Daniel** (*laughs*) No.

**Joe** (*half-laughs*) Yeah.

*Daniel exits, laughing, shaking his head. Joe watches
him go. Pause. Joe looks around. Joe thinks. Beat. He
decides something. Daniel re-enters.*

Alright?

**Daniel** Yeah.

**Joe** So what like what's . . .

**Daniel** Can you keep a secret?

*Beat.*

**Joe** Yeah what?

*Beat.*

**Daniel** Well don't go . . . blabbing but . . . but I actually
prefer . . . but I actually more prefer to spend time, with
you . . . much more . . . much more better than I do . . .
than I do with Jonathan.

*Beat.*

**Joe** Yeah.

**Daniel** You're a nice guy.

*Beat.*

**Joe** You know that.

**Daniel** I mean, I mean Jonathan's alright but . . .

**Joe** Yeah he's . . . (*Beat.*) You see me like I ain't seen
Jonathan . . . for . . . little bit a' time still, y'know It's . . .

**Daniel** Well you're lucky then.

**Joe** Yeah?

**Daniel** Because I have to see him every day.

**Joe** (*half-laughs*) Yeah, fuck that like. 'ckin hell.

**Daniel** What would you, actually be doing, now. (*Beat.*)
On a normal day.

*Beat.*

**Joe** Boy . . . every day's different like.

**Daniel** Yeah.

**Joe** Like *Playdays*. Could be the . . . tent stop could be
the . . . patch stop. Remember *Playdays*?

**Daniel** Erm . . . I can hardly remember.

**Joe** Yeah it doesn't matter doesn't matter /

**Daniel** I would normally be doing . . . nothing.

**Joe** Nothing?

*Pause.*

**Daniel** Well Mum says . . . Well Mum says that . . . next
week, me and her should actually go down, to Camden
Community College.

**Joe** OK.

**Daniel** To book me in on a course down there.

**Joe** OK.

*Beat.*

**Daniel** But I don't actually want to do that. (*Beat.*) I'm
not actually interested in . . . I'm not actually interested
in, in Down's syndrome. (*Beat.*) I just . . . I just want to
be *me*. (*Beat.*) That's all.

*Beat.*

**Joe** Well that's . . . like . . . We can /

**Daniel** And Jonathan does get . . . quite impatient with me sometimes.

**Joe** He does.

**Daniel** But it's not my fault.

**Joe** Yeah John's . . . alright. Y'know? Up to a f– . . . point. (*Beat.*) But after that . . .

**Daniel** I actually just . . . don't really like him sometimes /

**Joe** Yeah people like that . . . you nah' a' mean you can't . . .

**Daniel** D'you mean, d'you mean you can't, erm, D'you mean you actually can't, trust them?

**Joe** That's what I'm talking about like you can't . . .

**Daniel** Yeah.

**Joe** You can't tr– I mean you say a' them . . .

**Daniel** Do you think, that you could trust someone like erm, that you could trust someone like . . . Harry Potter?

   *Beat.*

**Joe** Harry P– . . . Course man He's . . . on the level like /

**Daniel** Or Hermione?

**Joe** They're . . . different thing. (*Beat.*) But your brother . . .

**Daniel** I hate him.

   *Beat.*

**Joe** That's it.

**Daniel** I hate Dad, and I hate him. (*Beat.*) He's a lit– He's a lit– He's a lit– . . . He's a little dick-in-the-bum.

**Joe** (*half-laughs*) Is that – Is that what he is?

**Daniel** It actually feels like . . . you and me are brothers. (*Beat.*) And not him. (*Beat.*) I mean I know . . . I've only just met you but /

**Joe** No what you talking about we go way back don't we like We seen each other . . .

**Daniel** Yeah.

**Joe** . . . around.

**Daniel** Yeah. (*Beat.*) You're a nice guy.

**Joe** And you're . . . So are you.

**Daniel** (*smiles*) Do you think so?

**Joe** Course.

**Daniel** Thanks.

**Joe** We should do stuff shouldn't we.

**Daniel** Cool.

**Joe** Together.

**Daniel** Nice one.

**Joe** What d'you wanna do like what's . . .

    *Beat.*

**Daniel** Well.

**Joe** Yeah?

**Daniel** Well we could go and see the film of . . . of Harry Potter / again

**Joe** No not like that like I mean real stuff What d'you wanna . . .

**Daniel** (*half-laughs*) I don't really know what you mean.

*Pause. Joe half-laughs.*

**Joe** What How old are you . . . now twenty-five?

**Daniel** Yeah I am.

*Beat.*

**Joe** What and you wanna be living at home . . . with your mum . . . and your brother all your life is that the way you wanna be?

*Pause.*

You can hit Jonathan . . . straight back. You see me? (*Beat.*) Say your mum, and your dad . . . and your brother. (*Beat.*) Say you didn't have to worry about them. (*Beat.*) What would you do?

*Pause.*

We could go away.

*Beat.*

**Daniel** Wh– Where to?

**Joe** Seaside.

**Daniel** Cool.

**Joe** Up the beach. Fish 'n' chips.

**Daniel** Nice one.

**Joe** Nice one. JD's and Coke. Floss it out y'know?

**Daniel** What just, What just me and you?

**Joe** 'F you want.

*Beat.*

**Daniel** Yeah I'd like that.

**Joe** Yeah so would I.

**Daniel**  Yeah so would I.

**Joe**  And when you go away. (*Beat.*) Sometimes, if you have a nice time. (*Beat.*) Sometimes, you don't have to come back.

*Pause.*

**Daniel**  Yeah.

*Beat.*

**Joe**  Right. (*Beat.*) I tell you what we should do. Have you got a mobile phone Daniel?

**Daniel**  Yeah but it's not, it's not for all the time though because, because money doesn't grow on trees /

**Joe**  Yeah f– Tell me about it What I'm gonna do, I'm gonna give you my number, and I'll take yours . . .

**Daniel**  Yeah.

**Joe**  And we can do suttin soon and I'll give you a bell OK?

**Daniel**  OK.

*Pause.*

**Joe**  OK you ready?

**Daniel**  OK.

**Joe**  OK the number is 07 946 –

*Blackout.*

## ELEVEN

*November.*
*The living room at Jonathan's house. Sean and Susan.*
*Night. Fireworks going off outside. Pause. A big volley of*
*fireworks goes off nearby, and we hear children shouting.*

**Susan** (*sighs*) I can't stop . . . looking at the / phone

**Sean** Well he's chosen the right night to . . .

**Susan** Yes, / quite We can't deny his . . . sense of timing

**Sean** go gallivanting off anyway

**Susan** obviously it runs in the family /

**Sean** Well look Well Helen . . .

**Susan** As I've told you before /

**Sean** Yes, Yes you've / rung

**Susan** I've rung her several ti– All the possible . . .

**Sean** And probably . . . y'know as I say y'know /

*Susan sighs.*

**Sean** He is most probably . . . I am very hungry /

**Susan** Oh dear /

**Sean** He'll be watching the fireworks /

**Susan** If you . . . If you had be– If you had seen, the way
he has behaved for the last month / then I think you
would be more

**Sean** Oh come on now let's /

**Susan** I think you would be rather more . . . concerned /
about his whereabouts

**Sean** Daniel is . . . He's not / an idiot y'know

83

**Susan**  He's . . . Not speaking for for days and then . . . pissing in the washing machine, baking his Mars bars, smearing /

**Sean**  Pissing in the . . . And Jon– Jonathan is . . . at the / library?

**Susan**  Jonathan is at the library Yes he's just tottled off to the library He thinks for some reason he'll find his brother at the library /

**Sean**  Well if Danny goes . . . to the library then perhaps /

**Susan**  Oh don't pretend to be any more . . . stupid than you already are /

**Sean**  He'll be alright /

**Susan**  He will not be alright he will be . . . cold /

**Sean**  Oh Are you sure there's nothing in the / fridge?

**Susan**  Three and half – He He was supposed to be back at six Sean He could be sat in some . . . paedophile ring for all / we know

**Sean**  Oh quite Yes Here we go I mean if the paedophiles ha– Or hijacked by . . . terrorists /

**Susan**  Oh . . . Yes this / is

**Sean**  Or perhaps he is a terrorist /

**Susan**  This is absolutely / classic

**Sean**  (*laughs*) I mean Christ / almighty woman

**Susan**  'Let's send him here Let's send him there' Is it not a long way to g– 'Of course not He'll be alright' /

**Sean**  Can I, Can I speak now Can I . . .

*Susan moves away. Beat.*

And the f– . . . traffic getting here / y'know

84

**Susan**  Oh do shut up /

**Sean**  Stuck in . . . football . . . traffic all along /

*The sound of keys in a lock. Jonathan enters.*

/ John.

**Susan**  Where the fuck have you been?

**Jonathan**  What you ta– What you talking / about I been looking for him I been to the library I been to the swimming pool

**Susan**  The commu– The communication / in this family is absolutely appa–

**Sean**  Well look Well let's /

**Susan**  You were supposed to be quickly bloody checking then coming straight / back

**Jonathan**  Oh f– Calm yourself down Please /

**Susan**  Calm down?

**Sean**  Let's /

**Susan**  Calm down?

**Sean**  Let's not try / to

**Susan**  (*exiting*) Oh I can't believe the pair of you.

**Sean**  Oh . . .

**Susan**  (*off*) Idiots. Idiots.

**Jonathan**  (*to Sean*) Welcome back.

*Sean laughs. Beat.*

Long time no see.

*Beat.*

**Sean**  Yes. Yes It's been /

**Jonathan** Take your coat off.

*Beat. Sean starts taking his jacket off. Beat.*

She didn't wanna . . . get you over here. Y'know I made her . . . call you.

*Beat.*

**Sean** Well that's /

**Jonathan** Has Mum, told you. (*Beat.*) The way Danny's been?

*Beat.*

**Sean** Danny . . . Obviously Danny has become . . .

*Beat.*

**Jonathan** What? (*Beat.*) Danny has become what? (*Beat.*) He won't listen to me. Because he wants to make his own decisions. That's what he wants to do. (*Beat.*) So what do we do? (*Beat.*) Professor?

**Sean** Danny . . . obviously . . . Danny . . . wants to live . . . his life, of course, but he can't, he can live . . . *a* life . . . the contents of which must be . . . dictated, naturally by . . . by those that care for him and . . . (*Beat.*) And perhaps some of those . . . that care for him very much have been . . . neglectful in their . . . responsibilities Certainly I . . . (*Beat.*) Certainly I, will . . . be there. For him. (*Beat.*) In whatever way I . . .

*Beat.*

**Jonathan** I got . . . suttin for you I . . .

*Jonathan produces the photo from the first scene.*
*Beat.*

Meant to give it you back. (*Beat.*) She looks nice What's her name?

*Beat.*

**Sean** She's . . .

*Beat.*

**Jonathan** (*getting his phone out*) Well you've been . . . having a good time anyway like least someone has /

**Sean** Her name . . . (*Beat.*) Is Rachel She's really none of your business . . . / Jonathan

**Jonathan** (*texting on his phone*) Yeah what is my . . . What is my business I dunno If I . . . know any more /

**Susan** (*re-entering, noticing photo*) Well that was a lot of bloody use Who's she? Oh on second th– I don't think I want to – Put her away / whoever she is

**Sean** Oh Jonathan is /

**Susan** Jonathan seems to be . . . preoccupied with his phone as usual /

**Jonathan** I'm not preo– I got a text, from someone

**Susan** (*laughs*) Oh well from Danny from what? /

**Jonathan** From so– From someone, who might know where he is.

**Susan** Who?

*Beat.*

**Jonathan** Oh it doesn't / matter

**Susan** Yes it / does bloody matter It matters to me

**Sean** Oh come on . . . Jonathan /

**Jonathan** From Jo– I get a text, from Joe.

*Beat.*

**Susan** Joe?

*Jonathan sighs.*

**Susan** Joseph / Warren Are you trying to tell me

**Sean** Well hang on a minute Who's J– Who's Joe? /

**Susan** you're still hanging around with him?

**Jonathan** I'm not ha– I don't see him any more I thought he might know where he is because . . . But he doesn't anyway because he just told me so that's that.

**Susan** Well I . . . struggle to think why Joseph Warren should possibly know where Danny is /

**Jonathan** He's /

**Sean** Who is / Joseph . . .

**Jonathan** Oh /

**Susan** You know who he is He's the hooligan who / who

**Jonathan** I mean even if I had been . . . hanging around wi– I mean you'd never notice anyway /

**Susan** I beg your pardon? /

**Jonathan** Cos you never . . . And Danny's . . . voted with his fucking feet hasn't he /

**Sean** Well look well obviously . . . Danny's behaviour has deteriorated and this is something that I . . . wasn't / aware of

*Jonathan laughs.*

**Susan** Well of course you're not aware of it You've buggered off I spend my days . . . wading through . . . shit /

*Jonathan sighs.*

for the benefit of you, and the benefit of Daniel

**Jonathan** / Danny

**Susan** A woman . . . da– bashes her . . . three-year-old . . . son over the head then tries to drown him, then I come home to a . . . eighteen-year-old who can barely look at me, and a twenty-five-year-old toddler who wets the bed and watches Harry fucking Potter /

**Sean** Can we all, just /

*The door bell goes. Jonathan and Susan both move to get it, but Susan gets there first – she exits.*

Well this'll be him . . . now you see this'll . . .

*Beat.*

**Jonathan** Maybe you were right. (*Beat.*) Y'know to send him away. (*Beat.*) Like When he was born. (*Beat.*) Dad. (*Beat.*) You must a' thought y'know. (*Beat.*) I mean Come on. (*Beat.*) You can say. (*Beat.*) Y'know We'd all . . . (*Beat.*) You can say.

*Beat. Susan enters, followed by Lauren.*

**Susan** Lauren's here.

**Sean** (*to Susan*) Did you not . . . Did you not think about . . . asking him . . . if he wanted to go to the fireworks? *

**Lauren** Y'alright?

*Beat.*

**Jonathan** Yeah I'm alright What you d– . . . You didn't have to come round here you . . .

**Lauren** (*shrugs*)

**Susan** * Oh don't be bloody stupid Where's my mobile?

*Beat.*

**Jonathan** This is my dad.

**Sean** Hi.

*Beat.*

**Jonathan** This is Lauren.

**Lauren** Hello.

**Sean** Nice to meet / you

**Susan** You keep your hands to yourself

**Sean** I /

**Susan** (*on mobile*) He– Hello Helen? Hello . . .

*Susan exits, followed by Sean.*

**Jonathan** Joe's . . . text me.

*Beat.*

**Lauren** To say what?

*Beat.*

**Jonathan** (*shaking his head*) I . . .

*Beat. He shows her the text.*

Lost suttin. Have you lost suttin.

*Beat.*

**Lauren** Well what's that mean?

*Beat.*

**Jonathan** Well I dunno What d'you think it means? /

**Lauren** Well I dunno What d'you think it means? /

*Sean re-enters.*

**Sean** Oh . . . Danny you . . .

*Jonathan's phone bleeps to indicate a new text message, as Susan re-enters.*

**Susan**  Well I've checked and double-checked and no one has . . . Anyone who . . . might possibly have . . . seen him . . .

*Beat.*

**Lauren**  D'you want a cup of tea Susan?

*Beat.*

**Susan**  I'd . . . Yes I'd / think I'd

**Sean**  Good idea /

**Jonathan**  I think we hav– . . . Call – I think we have to call the police.

**Sean**  What? Jonath– Slow /

**Jonathan**  I get a / te– I get another . . .

**Susan**  What are you – What's the matter? /

**Jonathan**  (*giving her the phone*) It's Joe. It's J– It's Joe It's f– It's my fault /

**Susan**  What on earth d'you– I can't understand what on earth this means /

**Jonathan**  It's a text, from Joe He's . . . Danny's . . .

**Sean**  Jonathan what's going on / here

**Jonathan**  I f– I fell out . . . with Joe . . . in the summer We f– /

**Lauren**  We had some trouble with / Joe like

**Jonathan**  I think he might a' done . . . taken or done . . . / summink to

**Sean**  Well what's Joe got /

**Jonathan**  I think Danny might be with Joe. (*Beat.*) Y'know?

*Beat.*

**Sean**  Oh f– . . . /

**Susan**  Phone the police.

**Sean**  Yes. Right. Yes.

**Susan**  Well what are you waiting for?

**Sean**  Well d– Does anyone know the number?

**Jonathan**  / 999 Dad it is . . .

**Susan**  999 you fucking cretin What d'you think it is?

**Sean**  I need the number, for Islington poli– Oh here we are Yes I see someone's . . . helpfully sellotaped it to the phone here I think it was me if I / remember correctly

**Susan**  Oh Just / Just f–

**Sean**  (*dialling*) 7, 607

**Susan**  (*to Jonathan*) How many . . . messages have you had from this . . .

**Jonathan**  Two just . . . two /

**Susan**  (*to Sean*) He's had two of these . . . You have to tell them He's had two of these / things

**Sean**  Look I will te– I'm in a queue here . . . y'know I'm in a queue to speak to the coppers /

**Susan**  Oh give it to me

*Sean exits, followed by Susan.*
*Jonathan sighs.*

**Susan**  (*off*) What are you doing?

**Jonathan**  He might / kill him. *

**Sean**  (*off*) Oh will you please just . . .

92

**Susan** (*off*) Come here.

**Sean** (*off*) Hello? Hello I need to repo–

*A door slams shut.*

**Lauren** * He won't kill him. (*Beat.*) He'll scare him.

*Beat.*

**Jonathan** It's my fault. (*Beat.*) Remember all that stuff I to– I'm a shit . . . brother I always have / been

**Lauren** He /

**Jonathan** I'm sorry Dan. Sorry Dan.

**Lauren** He loves you.

*Beat.*

**Jonathan** Well that's a big . . . problem then isn't it cos if I, can't . . .

*Beat. Susan re-enters, followed by Sean.*

**Susan** Well your father's going to go to the . . . police station Now I think you and I should go to Joseph's house /

**Jonathan** Joseph's h– He's not . . . living anywhere He's /

**Susan** Oh good / grief

**Sean** No let J– John should come with me. Go and ring Helen and tell her to come round

**Susan** Oh don't start . . . mothering me you . . . cretinous idiot

*Susan exits, followed by Lauren.*

**Lauren** (*exiting*) Susan I can stay round here if you wanna go.

*Beat.*

**Sean** (*to Jonathan*) It'll be OK.

**Jonathan** Will it.

*Pause.*

I can't be like you. (*Beat.*) I can't.

*Beat.*

**Sean** (*exiting*) I'll get the car.

**Susan** (*off*) Sean, Go.

**Sean** (*off*) I'm going.

*We hear the front door slam. Jonathan picks up Danny's drawing of a heart. He stares at it.*

**Susan** (*off, phone*) Danny darling please pick up the phone It's Mummy. It's . . . wherever you are . . .

*A door slams. Loud fireworks start going off outside. Lauren re-enters. She watches Jonathan. He is whispering to himself.*

**Jonathan** I'll be better. (*Beat.*) I'll be bet- . . . (*Beat.*) I'll be good. (*Beat*) I . . .

*Pause. Blackout.*


TWELVE

*December.*
*An allotment, in the shadow of Heathrow Airport.*
*Lauren enters. She tosses a pair of keys up in the air and catches it. She watches a plane taking off overhead.*

**Daniel** (*off*) And what, and what else?

**Jonathan** (*off*) And er . . . And 'Jingle Bells. Batman smells'.

94

**Daniel** (*off*) And what else?

**Jonathan** (*off*) And . . . and 'Away in a Manger'.

**Daniel** (*off*) And what else?

**Lauren** Come on boys I'm freezing out here / man

**Jonathan** (*off*) Come on boy she's freezing out here man.

*Jonathan and Daniel enter. Daniel is blindfolded.*

**Daniel** (*laughing, as he enters*) Stop copying, what people / say

**Jonathan** What people say (*To Lauren.*) Cool?

**Lauren** Cool.

**Jonathan** Cool.

**Daniel** Are we actually there yet?

**Jonathan** Right. Stop. Left turn.

**Lauren** (*waving her hand in front of him*) Can you see this Daniel?

**Daniel** See what?

**Lauren** Look at the view man.

**Jonathan** He can't can he – Right. Kneel down.

**Daniel** (*kneeling down*) Well what, Well what for? /

**Lauren** (*to Jonathan*) What you doing?

**Jonathan** (*looking at Lauren*) You kneeling down?

**Daniel** Where are we?

*Beat.*

**Jonathan** Guantánamo Bay Dan. We're gonna give you to the Americans.

**Daniel** What?

*Jonathan laughs.*

**Lauren** Jonathan.

**Jonathan** I'm only j– No it's alright Danny Get up, get up. That's the one.

**Daniel** I don't know when – I don't know when – I don't know when you're being serious, or when you're joking.

**Jonathan** No neither do I.

**Lauren** (*starting to take off his blindfold*) Your brother's a dickhead Danny you know that?

**Daniel** (*smiling*) Yeah I kn– Yeah I know / that

**Jonathan** Don't f– listen to a word, she / says

**Lauren** Here we go. You ready?

**Daniel** Yeah I'm ready.

*She finishes removing the blindfold.*

**Jonathan** Ta-da. And all that . . . bollocks.

*Beat.*

**Lauren** Woy What d'you reckon?

**Jonathan** He's . . . speechless, obviously.

**Lauren** What d'you think? Danny? (*Beat.*) Bit cold innit.

**Jonathan** Never mind the c– . . . (*Beat.*) Dan?

*Pause.*

**Daniel** What, actually is this place?

*Lauren looks at Jonathan, laughing. Beat.*

**Jonathan** Well. It is what you might call. An allotment.

**Daniel** An allotment?

**Jonathan** That's the one.

*Lauren laughs.*

That's the one.

**Daniel** Wow.

**Lauren** (*pointing*) And that's one over there, That's one over there /

**Jonathan** And this one, is . . .

**Lauren** Your one mate.

**Daniel** Is it, Is it all mine?

**Jonathan** You fucking, You better believe it This is your . . . Christmas present bruv.

**Daniel** Is it a Christmas present?

**Jonathan** That's what I said.

*Beat.*

**Daniel** But it's not actually Christmas / until

**Lauren** Yeah /

**Jonathan** Yeah I know it's . . . few days . . . early but . . .

**Lauren** Surprises.

**Jonathan** Surprises.

**Lauren** Come nice innit Danny What d'you reckon? Ha?

*Beat.*

**Daniel** I actually think, that this is really, really, amazing.

**Lauren** Oh we thought you would.

*Daniel hugs her. She laughs.*

We thought you would Daniel /

**Jonathan**  Oi. Happy Christmas Danny put it there.

*Jonathan offers his hand. As Daniel moves to accept it Jonathan puts it to his nose and sticks his tongue out.*

Ah-ah too slow mu'fucker No I'm only joking here you go.

*He embraces him, pats him on the back.*

That's better.

**Lauren**  What d'you say?

**Daniel**  Thanks.

**Jonathan**  You're welcome.

*Beat.*

**Lauren**  (*to Jonathan*) He's alright though in' he like.

**Daniel**  Yeah he is.

**Jonathan**  He is.

**Lauren**  'S 'bout time . . . he got you suttin nice though innit /

**Jonathan**  What a f– liberty D'you hear that Danny I tell you what I'm seeing another side to you.

**Lauren**  Oh yeah?

**Jonathan**  Oh yeah.

**Daniel**  What's that place over there?

**Jonathan**  Oh . . .

**Lauren**  That's the airport.

**Daniel**  Is it really?

**Jonathan**  Yeah it really is.

**Daniel**  (*to Lauren*) Did you . . . actually used to work there?

**Lauren** Yeah we both did didn't we That's how he got . . . this place.

**Jonathan** I'm a connected guy.

**Daniel** (*smiling*) No, No you're not You're, You're a wanker.

**Lauren** (*laughing*) That's right Danny / You know this

**Jonathan** Fucking cheek.

**Lauren** That's exactly what he is.

**Daniel** Put it there.

*He holds out his palm. She gives him a high-five.*

**Lauren** Yes my ute.

**Daniel** And another one.

*She gives him another one.*

And another one.

**Jonathan** No not another one Dan she'll get . . . excited Look at that plane.

**Daniel** Well what – Well what plane?

**Lauren** That plane /

**Jonathan** Shh.

*They watch a plane take off. Beat.*

**Daniel** That's, amazing.

**Jonathan** Have to get used to them.

**Lauren** Look a' that view Danny. (*Beat.*) Yeah?

**Daniel** It actually looks quite pretty.

**Lauren** Yeah.

*Beat.*

**Daniel**  Like you do.

**Jonathan**  Come over here Dan I wanna show you suttin.

**Daniel**  (*coming over*) Well what, Well what is it?

**Jonathan**  This, is, soil. Yes? (*Beat.*) And whatever you do . . . down here . . . you always need, soil.

**Daniel**  Yeah I kn– Yeah I know that.

**Jonathan**  Good. Now I need your help on this.

**Daniel**  (*laughing*) Shut up.

**Jonathan**  Come on here we go.

*They start spreading some soil around, and Jonathan starts unwrapping a plant or seeds.*

**Lauren**  (*with phone*) I get full bars out here like Why don't I get any . . . round my house /

**Daniel**  What are you doing?

*Beat.*

**Jonathan**  See you put . . . a seed down. In the earth don't you.

**Daniel**  Yeah.

*Beat.*

**Jonathan**  And you water it and . . . water it and . . . (*Beat.*) Might take months. (*Beat.*) And years . . . (*Beat.*) But I'm gonna be here. (*Beat.*) Y'know sometimes I might be . . . away y'know who knows.

**Daniel**  Yeah.

*Beat.*

**Jonathan**  But I'll always come back. (*Beat.*) And we'll watch it all growing. (*Beat.*) We'll be two old men together won't we.

**Daniel**  Yeah we will be.

**Jonathan**  Yeah.

*Beat.*

**Daniel**  But what, but what about Lauren though?

*Lauren smiles. Beat.*

**Jonathan**  Yeah and Lauren y'know.

**Daniel**  Cool.

*Beat.*

**Jonathan**  She can make the tea.

**Lauren**  I heard that.

**Jonathan**  I know.

**Daniel**  Can I ask you something?

**Jonathan**  What.

*Beat.*

**Daniel**  What's actually happened, to Joe?

*Beat.*

(*To Lauren.*) Because, because one night, I was supposed to go and meet him, and we were supposed to go and live . . . And we were supposed to go to the seaside.

**Lauren**  Oh . . .

**Daniel**  But he didn't actually turn up.

**Lauren**  Yeah well. (*Beat.*) I wouldn't wanna live by the seaside would you?

**Daniel**  Not really no.

**Lauren**  Boring.

**Daniel** I just feel like . . . I just feel like I let him down, that's all /

**Jonathan** Yeah you don't have to worry about . . . Joe. (*Beat.*) Any more.

*Beat.*

**Daniel** At the weekend, I actually decided a few things.

**Lauren** Oh yeah?

**Daniel** I actually decided, that I'm not going to go, to Londis any more. Because, because the people in there are too rude, and they never smile.

**Lauren** (*smiles*) Yeah *waste* like.

**Daniel** And I'm also . . . going to clean my teeth *after* breakfast, as well as before.

**Jonathan** Good call.

**Lauren** That's good.

**Daniel** (*to Lauren*) Can I ask you something?

**Lauren** Yeah what's that?

*Beat. Daniel sighs.*

**Daniel** I don't wanna sound . . . personal or anything . . .

**Jonathan** (*quietly*) Oh God.

**Daniel** But when you do your singing. (*Beat.*) Does it actually make you go . . . Does it actually make you go warm, inside. Does it actually make you go warm inside?

*Beat.*

**Lauren** Er . . . Sometimes yeah, I guess.

**Jonathan** She's got a studio booked in the New Year.

**Daniel** Have you really?

**Lauren** (*nods*) Yep, yep.

*Beat.*

**Daniel** Are you two, actually gonna get married or something?

*Lauren laughs.*

**Jonathan** Not this minute.

**Daniel** Well you should do.

**Jonathan** Yeah well.

**Daniel** I actually think, I actually think you make a really good couple.

**Jonathan** Oh well that's sorted then.

**Daniel** Not like Mum and Dad but, but better.

**Jonathan** Do your jacket up.

**Daniel** Yeah al*right.*

*Daniel moves away and starts digging around with a little spade. Lauren moves over to Jonathan. He holds her. Beat.*

**Jonathan** D'you think I'm alright?

**Lauren** I think you're an idiot.

*Beat.*

**Jonathan** Yeah?

**Lauren** Yeah.

*Beat.*

**Jonathan** Oh well that's alright then Oi Dan, Danny.

**Daniel** What?

*Beat.*

**Jonathan**  I can be your gardener like You can employ me.

**Daniel**  What? Oh.

*Beat.*

**Jonathan**  How much you gonna pay me?

**Lauren**  Don't listen to him.

**Daniel**  Tw– twenty pounds.

**Jonathan**  Yeah?

*Beat.*

**Daniel**  A hundred.

**Jonathan**  Wow.

*A plane is passing low overhead. Beat.*

Gimme a bell in the New Year We'll sort it out. (*Beat.*) Got my number?

*Pause.*

Yeah I need . . . (*Beat.*) Something.

*Daniel carries on messing around in the soil. Jonathan looks out at the view. Lauren takes his hand. Pause. Music. Lights fade.*

*The End.*

# UNDERCARRIAGE

**Undercarriage** was first performed during a young people's theatre festival at Birmingham Rep on 30 March 2007, directed by Ben Payne. Stephanie was played by Catherine Skinner, and Billy Dosanjh was The Body.

**Stephanie**
White. Fourteen years old, from Birmingham.

The present.

*Dark.*

*Piano music plays, quietly.*
    *Then, the sound of an aeroplane passing low overhead. Getting louder and louder as it gets nearer, then fading.*

### ONE

*Lights up on: an old barn, in the countryside near Birmingham Airport. Light streams in from an open doorway.*
    *A teenage girl, Steph. She wears school uniform. She stares ahead. She is breathing heavily, and has been crying.*
    *Pause.*
    *She slowly looks around the barn, then looks back at the open doorway. She stares at it. Pause.*
    *Blackout.*

### TWO

*Lights up on: a few minutes later. She is in a corner, being sick. She finishes. She paces aimlessly. She goes over to her bag, kneels down and produces some tissues – she wipes her mouth. She finishes. Pause. She gets her phone out, hesitates, looking towards the door. She throws her phone in her bag – as it lands. Blackout.*

## THREE

*Lights up on: Steph pacing slowly around. She is muttering to herself, having an argument with someone in her head. She is barely audible.*

Just f– . . . Just f– . . . found him Well I don't know do I?

*She is imitating her mother.*

'Why didn't you t– phone the poli–' Well I don't f– . . . bloody . . .

*She sighs. Looks towards the doorway, then starts pacing again, whispering.*

Doesn't matter doesn't matter.

Doesn't matter.

*Pause. She stares ahead, thinking. A smile breaks across her face – she laughs. She paces again, looking towards the doorway, smiling, shaking her head.*
*Her phone vibrates in her pocket. She stops. She gets it out. She stares at the number flashing up. She allows it to ring and ring until it rings off. Pause. She looks towards the doorway. The phone vibrates to indicate a new voice message. She stares at it. She is about to put it to her ear, then stops. Pause. She presses the phone against her nose, thinking.*
*Blackout.*


## FOUR

*Lights up on: Steph, sitting down. She has an iPod earphone stuck out of one ear, and her phone stuck to the other. Pause.*

(*On phone.*) H– . . . Hiya Pauline it's Steph it's Stephanie.

(*Half-laughs.*) Not, not so bad thanks Is m– . . .

(*Laughs.*) Oh, oh you do as well. You do as well. Lis–, is Nana there? Thanks.

    *Pause.*

Hiya Na– Hiya Nana it's Stephanie.

Hi.

How are y– I'm alright how are you?

Yeah?

Why?

Oh Nana.

Oh your poor thing.

Oh I feel sorry for ya.

Oh I feel sorry for you I do.

Yeah.

Oh I'm alright. No I'm j– I'm out, at the erm . . . piano lessons.

(*Laughs.*) Really good yeah really good, erm . . . She's a bit . . . mad, erm . . . Listen I j– . . . There's summat I gotta erm . . .

Yeah I had to get two buses. Yeah I had t– Yeah I had to get two buses Listen y'know erm . . . if erm . . .

Yeah I had to get two buses. Yeah– Nana. It's just . . .

    *She is looking towards the doorway.*

I've . . . it's I've . . .

Oh it doesn't matter it's, I was just . . . Oh I'd better go the bus is . . . I'm waiting for the b– the bus is coming now. OK I will do. OK I'll give you a ring. OK bye. Bye.

*Hangs up. She sighs. Hesitates. She quickly writes and sends a text message. She looks towards the doorway. She exits.*

*Pause.*

*She re-enters, slowly, dragging something in with her. Eventually we can see it is the body of a dark-skinned man – dead. She has trouble dragging it in, but she slowly manages it. She stops, out of breath. She stares down at the body. Pause.*

*Blackout.*


### FIVE

*Piano music plays.*

*Lights up on: minutes later. Music continues. She is sitting near the body. She is staring at it. A book of piano music is open at her feet.*

*Pause.*

*She moves to touch the body, then stops.*

*Pause.*

*She lightly touches the body's face, then stops.*

*Pause. Blackout.*


### SIX

*Later. The body is now covered by a jacket, so we can't see its face.*

*Steph is on the phone, talking happily.*

– but I don't wanna do it She wanted me a' do it I didn't ask to do it. And Dad. Who never says anything.

I know yeah exa– exactly. Exactly.

Fucking piano lessons.

*On 'piano' she starts laughing.*

Oh Naomi she's a right old bag. She looks like a werewolf.

Oh, When are you coming back?

Yeah I don't like . . . sitting on me own.

I do in . . . Maths, Geography, Science Well what does the doctor say?

*Pause.*

Come back. (*Beat.*) I don't . . . (*Sighs.*) Oh I'm in a right . . .

*She's looking over at the body.*

I got this . . . Listen I was . . . coming back from the . . .

Oh well don't go.

Oh tell 'em to wait tell 'em to wait. I'll tell 'em.

OK.

OK L– . . . Bye.

*Hangs up. Stares over at the body. Pause. She idly throws a twig at the body – hits it. Music. She slowly stands up. Picks up her bag. Blackout.*

### SEVEN

*Two days later. The body lies in the same place, jacket still covering it.*
*Pause.*
*Steph enters. Carries her school bag and a book of piano music. Stares at the body. Pause. She goes over and lifts the jacket, looking at his face. Pause. She starts to cover him up again, hesitates, then lets the jacket drop, leaving the face uncovered.*

*She starts taking her jacket and bag off. Eventually, she produces a sandwich from a lunchbox. She sits down and*

*starts eating, looking over at the body. She eats. Pause.*
*She half-smiles.*
  *Blackout.*


## EIGHT

*Later. She is pacing slowly around. She has an exercise*
*book in her hand, which she consults occasionally. She is*
*trying to memorise something from it.*
  *Pause. She mutters to herself.*

*Au, au weekend, Je vais . . . Dans . . . Dans le weekend . . .*
*Bonjour, bonjour.*

  *She looks at the body.*

*Bonjour. Bonjour. Bon-jour.*

*Je m'appelle Stephanie. Stephanie. J'ai, quatorze, ans.*
*J'habite dans . . . J'h– . . . J'habite à Birmingham, dans*
*le . . . au cen– . . . au centre d'Angleterre, qui est . . . Je*
*suis née. Née. Er, j'ai deux chats, qui s'appellent Sammy*
*et Garfield. Dans le weekend, je vais . . . shopping, avec*
*mes amis, et, quelquefois . . . aller à la . . . cinéma.*
*Cinéma. Cin-ém-a.*

  *She has moved right over to the body. She is smiling.*
  *She hesitates, then props the body up against the wall,*
  *struggling at first, but eventually managing it.*
    *Pause.*

*Bonjour.*

*Ça va?*

*Où est, you . . . from, Where, are you . . .*

  *She stops. She hesitates. Pause.*

*J'ai vu . . .*

*Pause.*

My name is Stephanie. I am fourteen years old. I was born . . . I have two cats . . .

*Pause.*

I saw . . . a man.

Falling from the sky.

From an aeroplane.

*Pause.*

And it was you.

*Pause. Blackout.*


## NINE

*Later. She's got some homework laid out in front of her, which she is doing, and talking to the body at the same time. She is pretending to be her piano teacher.*

Scales, are, the building blocks. OK? Bit like . . . if you don't know . . . your scales, you don't know your alphabet. Yes? So if– . . .

Well let's, well let's, well I understand what you're saying but perhaps if we just . . . for example with my alphabet I can form words, and from words I can form . . .

*She mimes some piano playing.*

Phrases. Yes? So from this . . .

*Mimes playing a scale.*

To this.

*Mimes playing a more intricate piece.*

OK? I mean obviously you won't be as good as . . . as
that but you have to take . . . you have to start . . .

*Her phone starts vibrating. She looks at it. Answers it
quickly.*

Hiya. H– Hi I was just gonna ring you.

Why what's up?

Oh my G– . . .

Well it can't be that . . . Well it can't b– . . .

Well what, well what do the doctors say?

Oh Naomi.

Well I'll come, well I'll come round.

Well I don't c– Visiting time's – . . . Well fuck visiting
time it's . . . I'm . . .

*She sighs. Piano music. Pause.*

Yeah.

Yeah.

Well don't be scared.

Don't be.

I– . . .

*Beat. Blackout.*


TEN

*Music continues. Lights up on: later, dark. She is pacing
near the body. She has been crying. She starts beating the
body, punching and kicking it. Stops. The sound of rain
from outside. Pause. Blackout.*

## ELEVEN

*A week later. She is sitting down near the body. Pause.*
*She half-laughs.*

Churches eh.

Big, old . . .

*Pause.*

Would you get married in a church?

I used to think . . . I'll never get married I won't.

I won't bother.

*Pause.*

I never knew she had so many uncles.

*Pause.*

I.

Have got a preliminary examination tomorrow.

*Pause.*

Which I'm gonna go to.

*She drinks some water, pleased with herself.*

Well enough about me what about you. You dead prick.
What about ya. Where, are you from.

What brings you here.

To me.

To mine.

*Pause.*

Time to go.

Don't you reckon?

*Pause. Blackout.*


### TWELVE

*Lights up on the body, alone in the darkness. The sound of Stephanie's voice, on a recording.*

My name's . . . My name is Stephanie Beech.

I am fourteen years old.

I have two cats.

I live at 32, Linx Drive. I was . . . it was the 22nd. Of October. I was walking f– . . . I was walking, from my piano lessons. Out there. Got a 2 . . . 12 bus from Solihull, and then a 38A from the Maypole.

I had a half-hour piano lesson . . . I was walking . . . back . . . to get the bus back into town, when I saw . . .

A plane came overhead. From . . . going to the airport. Towards it. And there was . . . I saw . . . out of it there was . . .

I ran . . . over. Maybe half . . . a mile.

And there he was.

The man had dark skin.

And he had blue jeans.

And . . . and a jacket.

And it was barely . . . scratched.

Even though he'd . . . fallen he was barely . . .

And there was a . . . barn and . . . I saw a barn and . . . so I took him in and . . . I saved him.

*Pause.*

He was dead.

Erm.

*Pause. The sound of a plane passing low overhead.
Blackout.*


### THIRTEEN

*Two days later. Lights up on: the barn, empty. After a bit,
we hear Stephanie, leaving a message on the phone.*

(*Off.*) – and it came through . . . today and it's distinction.

*She enters, on the phone, clutching a bottle of wine
and two glasses.*

Er . . . Distinction so that's . . . really good. Erm. So I'll
speak to you soon OK bye.

*She hangs up, and realises the place is empty. She
stops. Looks for the body. She stops. Pause. Blackout.*

*The End.*